Poetry Ireland Review 127

Eagarthóir / Editor
Eavan Boland

© Poetry Ireland Ltd 2019

Poetry Ireland Ltd/Éigse Éireann Teo gratefully acknowledges the assistance of The Arts Council/An Chomhairle Ealaíon and The Arts Council of Northern Ireland.

LOTTERY FUNDED

Poetry Ireland invites individuals and commercial organisations to become Friends of Poetry Ireland. For more details, please contact: Poetry Ireland Friends Scheme, Poetry Ireland, 11 Parnell Square East, Dublin 1, Ireland
or telephone +353 1 6789815; e-mail info@poetryireland.ie

FOUNDING PARTNERS
Adrian Brinkerhoff Poetry Fund of the Sidney E Frank Foundation

POETRY PATRONS: EPIC
Thomas Dillon Redshaw

POETRY PATRONS: LYRIC
Eithne Hand, Ruth Webster

POETRY PATRONS: SONNET
Neville Keery, Nana Lampton, William McConkey, Joan and Joe McBreen, Anonymous

POETRY PATRON: HAIKU
Ciara McCluskey

FRIENDS OF POETRY IRELAND
Desmond Windle, Rachel Joynt, Noel and Anne Monahan, Maurice Earls, Mary Shine Thompson, Seán Coyle, Andrew Caldicott, Henry and Deirdre Comerford

Poetry Ireland Review is published three times a year by Poetry Ireland Ltd. The Editor enjoys complete autonomy in the choice of material published. The contents of this publication should not be taken to reflect either the views or the policy of the publishers.

ISBN: 978-1-902121-75-8   ISSN: 0332-2998

PUBLICATIONS MANAGER: Paul Lenehan with Rachel Botha, with the assistance of Maddy Folstein, Anna Bonner, and Orla Higgins

DESIGN: Alistair Keady (www.hexhibit.com)
COVER CREDIT: *Laundry* (2018) by Amelia Stein RHA

Contents

Editorial

A few months ago, I came across a paragraph from a newspaper. It was from an article published in July 1962 in *The Evening Press*. The writer was Patrick Kavanagh. The purpose of his article was to announce the imminent publication of a literary magazine, *Poetry Ireland*, to be edited by John Jordan, a revival of David Marcus's *Poetry Ireland* from 1948. Kavanagh salted the information with the statement: 'In our own tin-pot way there is a disbelief that poetry has any value.'

We asked several poets to respond to his statement, and about how they feel poetry is valued now in Ireland. Tara Bergin, Chris Murray, Michael Longley, Vona Groarke, Toby Buckley, Chiamaka Enyi-Amadi, Stephen Sexton, Aifric Mac Aodha – all poets with different backgrounds and aesthetics – give the subject their eloquent attention.

In every generation poets have been invited to mirror a society's doubt. It almost has an allure. As if apologising for poetry could reassure the social order that the practitioner of an art was willing to disown it. But it makes no sense. In her excellent first lecture – 'Imaginary Bonnets with Real Bees in Them' – as Ireland Professor of Poetry, Paula Meehan spoke of the life of a poem in a memorable phrase, referring to a 'shadow power' in the 'ghost life of the word'. Who would want to take away that ghost life from people? Who would want to disown it? What would be the purpose of striking at the way a poem enters into people's lives?

And there's a larger question. What does a poet owe to poetry in their own time? Are they stewards and advocates, or simply that person who takes out a notebook after dark and struggles with the space? And by so doing makes a new one? There is no perfect answer, but the question is considered by different poets in different ways here, adding to the conversation we share and hand on.

– Eavan Boland

Teri Ellen Cross Davis

DON'T ACT LIKE A

On the train from Baltimore
a woman ignores her young son
until his boredom makes mischief fun
and her unengaged gaze narrows, sharpens
and we all hear the slap followed by words
meant to bruise, *Don't act like a faggot.*
Maybe years later he will kiss a man
and taste despair, maybe years later
he will kick a man to hide his own fear.
Maybe none of these things will happen.
But my own silence is cultivated by years
of attempted interventions met with
blistering invectives, my own verbal fumbles
trying not to judge, while judging.
I wonder how long it will take
to embrace a masculinity not drenched
in cowardice, its stench as strong as semen.
I wonder how many years until we learn
not disgust, the instant flippant rebuke,
but the joy of a boy dancing
in his sister's princess dress, how the frills
flounce as he runs down the hall.
The pink spaghetti straps framing square
shoulders waiting to broaden and fill.

Janis Woodgate

LADYBIRD

Hunker down to poke at the coals
turn each one over to redden the black
Make it go further, while drying the clothes
on the old horse's back –

and the rug and the couch and
the dog and the child and
yourself

Whoever spoke those syrupy
words in your ear, left
sticky trails

and castles and balls and
princes and forests and
feasts

Leading you
up the garden path

Leaving you
nothing but the crumbs.

Daniel Hardisty

CEDAR, SANDALWOOD, CUT STEMS

Those bulbs of rain, clear and time-slowed,
that fell as you shook out your umbrella.
The storefront lights still on in the high street.

The pitching, rain-fractaled headlamps
swooping the glass as we gave the address;
and the sudden scent of you, half yourself,

half perfume: like cedar, sandalwood,
cut stems, and the smell that lingers in rain
that ran so quick-fingered through me.

Iain Twiddy

THE BATHROOM WINDOW

Was there really an evening thirty years ago,
looking from my grandma's open bathroom window,
spring bulbing underneath, lilac light ascending
with the give of a boulder rolled away from a tomb;

with the water in the bath as dappled as the glass,
the silver brushes poised on her bedroom dresser
instrumental to the silence, like an unheard sigh
as the city eased, nuzzling its scent like a cat;

when the chunked-up lawn was less apple-crumbly,
and the alley wall as asking for the ping
of the plastic football as your shadow was itching
to find you, stride out again into the light;

was there really an evening when the cold tap spattered
and frothed like an iceberg bursting into thaw,
when the bits of tank in the bath retraced the bed
of the river kicked into swill and swirl in summer;

when that window was the sleeves of a jumper hoicked up,
the breeze like a finger you could draw here, or place there,
really an evening so opening like a window in me,
when ever since anything else could have happened.

Bernadette Ní Riada

CUIMHINÍGÍ ORAINN

From Parnell Square take the few steps into the garden.
Walk slowly
through the length of it.
Climb the steps.
Read the extract from Liam Mac Uistín's poem
that begins:

> *I ndorchacht an éadóchais rinneadh aisling dúinn.*
> *Lasamar solas an dóchais ...*
>
> In the darkness of despair we saw a vision.
> We lit the light of hope ...

Stand for a while with your back to the curved wall.
Walk down the steps.
Look up at the Children of Lir.
Take a picture.
Ensure you get the tricolour in.
Walk the length and breadth of the garden again.
Notice the boxes and boxes of blooming flowers,
the readers, smokers, feeders with paper bags on their laps.
Pick your own spot on one of the brown benches.
Stay awhile.
Gaze at the still water, imprisoned
in its concrete, cross-shaped trough.

Benjamin Keatinge

SAGAS DON'T CONFORM TO OUR DESIGN

Micheal O'Siadhail, *The Five Quintets* (Baylor University Press, 2018),
$34.95 hb.

When Micheal O'Siadhail resigned his research professorship at the Dublin
Institute for Advanced Studies to become a full-time poet in 1987, his
writing followed a new direction. As he informs us in his Introduction
to *Poems 1975-1995* (Bloodaxe Books, 1999), '[t]he quality of concentration
I could then afford made me move from collections united by an angle
of vision to books with an architecture, an overriding focus'. His latest
collection, *The Five Quintets* (2018), follows this architectonic turn and, in
doing so, it offers a panorama in poetry of (mainly) western intellectual
history covering five principal domains: '[a]rtistic creativity, economics,
politics, science' and philosophy / theology, broadly conceived as 'the
search for meaning in our lives'. This is a highly ambitious framework,
which is orchestrated under the headings: 'Making', 'Dealing', 'Steering',
'Finding', and 'Meaning', these being the five quintets of the title which
are themselves comprised by further subheadings. There are five Cantos
in each Quintet and the book extends to 375 pages of densely-packed verse.
Like most of O'Siadhail's previous collections of the post-1987 period,
including *The Gossamer Wall: Poems in Witness to the Holocaust* (2002), *Love
Life* (2005), *Globe* (2007), *Tongues* (2010), and *One Crimson Thread* (2015), this
book is highly schematic, and the poet makes a painstaking attempt to
encompass a broad swathe of the history of ideas, ancient and modern,
and in so doing, he provides a kind of intellectual dictionary of biography
which tells us 'what happened ... through [the] lives and personalities' of
major thinkers and social or political figures in the chosen domains of
endeavour.

Indeed, this is an epic poem, of sorts, taking its point of departure
(rather self-consciously, one feels) from both Dante – that universal
intellect of late medieval Europe – and TS Eliot, author of *Four Quartets*
(which itself consists of four sections – 'Burnt Norton', 'East Coker',
The Dry Salvages', and 'Little Gidding' – each subdivided into five parts).
O'Siadhail imagines his *Five Quintets* as an extension of this schema, 'A
fifth quartet – or should I say quintet?', as he suggests in Quintet 1, Canto
4, 'Breaking Out', v. There are also Miltonic echoes, for example in the
invocation to the Muse that begins Quintet 5, 'Meaning' ...

> You angel of the burning bush, inspire
> me now as I once more begin, and fan
> in me again a falling tongue of fire

... and also in the vastness of the enterprise which tries to justify the ways of both God and man, a sort of humanist/theological synthesis of intellectual history concluding with a paradise regained, a beatific vision:

> The angels turn to serving herbal teas –
> chrysanthemum, hibiscus, ginger root,
> hydrangea, camomile. As palates squeeze
>
> the tang and zing of blossom, plant or fruit,
> a mood of jokes and laughter now pervades
> the evening light that catches each minute
>
> detail. A feast of countless forms cascades
> the images each artist cries to know –
> a moment snatched in all its hues and shades.
>> – QUINTET 5, CANTO 5, 'BURNING BUSH', i

This is what O'Siadhail describes in the poem's Introduction as 'the joy and let-go of an imagined heaven', and it is one that he does not discern in Eliot's *Four Quartets* nor in the variegated vision of *The Divine Comedy* where paradise, the Introduction implies, lacks a human dimension. O'Siadhail's heaven aims to supply the human element while retaining the theological divine light. If, however, his version of the heavenly tea party appears more like a drawing room of inhibited Prufrockian gossip, then this may be because, as O'Siadhail acknowledges elsewhere in the poem, 'sagas don't conform to our design' (Quintet 1, Canto 5, 'Abundance', xi).

One may readily acknowledge the challenges of furnishing a transcendent vision on an epic canvas such as the one chosen for *The Five Quintets*. Our age is not naturally sympathetic, perhaps, to a Dantean paradisal culmination, a vision which Samuel Beckett described in terms of the 'static lifelessness of unrelieved immaculation', finding himself more attracted by the 'movement and vitality' of the *Purgatorio* ('Dante... Bruno. Vico.. Joyce'). But if Dante's *Paradiso* failed to win over Beckett, O'Siadhail likewise fails to convince the contemporary reader that his vision has overcome any of the 'lifelessness' of previous attempts to capture the divine in language. One might borrow a leaf from TS Eliot's *Four Quartets* which advocate a Beckettian 'ignorance' and 'dispossession' in the face of the modern world, reminding us that successful poetry is 'a raid on the inarticulate' ('East Coker'). It is the fluency of O'Siadhail's nicely-turned rhymes that ultimately grates with the reader. The poem has the same flaws that Philip Larkin identified in later Auden, a 'loss of vividness, a tendency to rehearse themes already existing as literature, a certain abstract windiness' ('What's Become of Wystan?', *Required Writing*). In the last analysis, *The Five Quintets* most resembles what Larkin characterises as the 'rambling intellectual stew' of Auden's *New Year Letter* (1941).

Within this somewhat indigestible panorama of human thought and deed, there is plenty to ponder and plenty of characterisations of individual thinkers and writers that are both striking and occasionally strange. O'Siadhail as vatic poet is something of a 'guiding Virgil' – Quintet 5, Canto 1, 'Word and Mind', iii – on a poetic journey which embraces and explicates the riffs of '*Madam Jazz*', who is the motif of a kind of free-wheeling encounter with the Yeatsian '*dance*' of the intellect and its 'imperfections' (opening invocation, '*Be with me, Madam Jazz, I urge you now*'). Whether one can indeed envisage Dietrich Bonhoeffer, Hannah Arendt, Said Nursî, Pope John XXIII, and Jean Vanier 'taking breakfast on a mezzanine' while they 'chat together' in 'unexpected friendship' (Quintet 5, Canto 5, 'Burning Bush', i), will depend on one's own poetic inclinations, but some may take umbrage at TS Eliot imagined in a haiku as a

> *Volt-sensitive shark*
> *A lumbering torpedo,*

who ...

> *Falls below the mark.*
> – QUINTET 1, CANTO 4, 'BREAKING OUT', V

And although O'Siadhail claims that Eliot's 'daring must fall short of paradise' (Quintet 1, Canto 4, 'Breaking Out', v), and therefore his 'great poem' *Four Quartets* is in need of 'a fifth part' (from the 'Introduction'), it remains evident that Eliot was uniquely sensitive among modern readers to the immaculate vision of Dante's *Paradiso*. In his essay, 'Dante' (1929), Eliot suggests that '[w]e have (whether we know it or not) a prejudice against beatitude as material for poetry', and argues that '[t]he *Paradiso* is not monotonous' but rather is 'as various as any poem'. Among the virtues that Eliot singles out in Dante's great poem are those of 'austerity' and 'economy' that enable the Italian to describe 'states of feeling' which are 'remote from ordinary experience' ('Dante', 1929). One welcomes the lucidity of Eliot's exposition just as one wonders if the juxtaposition of the ordinary 'breakfast on a mezzanine' with the extraordinary 'angels ... serving herbal teas' is entirely advisable in *The Five Quintets*. Rather, one feels that while Dante may have successfully integrated 'real men, his contemporaries, friends, and enemies, recent historical personages, legendary and Biblical figures' ('Dante', 1929) into the visionary fabric of his poem, one hesitates to affirm that the same symbiosis has been achieved by O'Siadhail.

The pleasures of this poem, such as they are, can be found mostly where it explores terrain less-frequented by the broader spectrum of poets now or at any time. If one may tend to become anaesthetised by 'the lamps of perfect rhyme' that O'Siadhail adopts, in words that describe French lyric poet Charles Baudelaire as a *'proud priest of the lyre'* (Quintet 1, Canto 2, 'Feeling Freed', v), one revives to some extent when lesser-known figures and their ideas enter the fray. Quintet 2 ('Making') introduces a host of famous and less-famous economists, including such figures as: Adam Smith, David Ricardo, John Stuart Mill, Karl Marx, Milton Friedman, Thorstein Veblen, and John Maynard Keynes, alongside our own Kerry-born economist, Richard Cantillon (1680-1732). It meditates on the boom and bust cycles that have historically plagued the world economy and it offers some admonitory contexts for Ireland's recent economic difficulties and the renewed signs of the Celtic Tiger's return. That said, certain phrases here and elsewhere are bound to antagonise the purist. Does the term 'exit strategy' sit comfortably in the poetic lexicon without the heavy irony of political satire (Quintet 3, Canto 1, 'Governance', i)? Or 'higgle-haggle of the mart' (Quintet 2, Canto 1, 'Mechanisms', ii)? Should we allow 'papist hocus-pocus laissez-faire' (Quintet 5, Canto 2, 'Binding and Freeing', i)? The answer will depend on your view of the 'poetry biz' and the 'soul's aha!' (Quintet 1, Canto 5, 'Abundance', xiii, xiv).

One wonders, finally, if the fluency and facility of *The Five Quintets* is really an apt response to the world around us. Certainly, other modern and contemporary poets (Eliot among them) have gone in an opposite direction to express their own inarticulacy in forms that are more troubled than the combination of regular stress and recognisable forms employed in this long poem. While these may partly be matters of taste and opinion, at the same time, in an expansive poem of design and ambition, one has to ask if its epic proportions are matched by its poetic accomplishment. And one is obliged to conclude that the match is imperfect.

Brian Cronwall

THE DOG WITH ONE BLUE EYE AND ONE BROWN EYE

> *... perdu comme ce chien*
> *Qui semble enfermé dans l'effroi d'une métempsycose*
> *Et qui flaire entre les jardins la trace de l'oubli.*

> ... lost like a dog
> That seems trapped in the fear of a metempsychosis
> And that sniffs between the gardens at forgetting's trace
> – Jacques Réda

Montpellier, France

The dog with one blue eye and one brown eye has lived
before. Looking in a pond, he sees a white coat
and thinks, for a moment, he remembers the sea,
a small abbey, a grandson he walked on wet sand;
then, a caterpillar becoming a monarch
butterfly crushed against a stone wall. But soon, he's
only, again, a dog, pausing at his cobbled
image before turning one blue eye and one brown
toward me, shaking his head, plodding across the square
down the Place de la Comédie, his tongue dripping,
toward his goal, the shadows near the fountain, and then,
looking at me for a moment, sniffs the air, sits,
lies down, weary, waiting for the next dream: winter,
a mountain pass, horses, snow, fog, a garden.

Ian Harrow

APPOINTMENT

As if I hadn't time enough,
I can reach the centre in five minutes or less.

When I eventually see
the nurse who takes the bloods

I think she's quite surprised
I'm not irritated by the delay

(I'm not irritated at all).
She wonders aloud if the last

half-full syringe will do
and laughs when I call my blood reluctant.

I commend her sunny room
which, however – she says – can make

it difficult to see the laptop screen.
How much time goes by in the silence

and a rush of things I nearly mention?
Directed to an unfamiliar exit

in the moment it takes to find out where I am
I decide to take the long way home

via the river and the refurbished café/library
and make an afternoon of it.

Katrina Naomi

WHAT ARRIVAL FEELS LIKE

Tugging the cold window down
I check myself, worried
I'll feel shy or regretful in some way, unsure
if the tears are caused by the rush of night
air, the thought of you, or the lights of Penzance –
their gaudy echo in the bay – or just my eyes' blur
after no sleep for 36 hours. The time has gone
backwards and forwards. I saw two sunsets
on an 11-hour flight – can that be possible?
I focus, as best I can, on the moon, the stars,
the end of the land, knowing I can travel
no further.
              I make believe I can see you,
way along the platform. After all these weeks,
I can. It's you in your green coat from Berlin,
I see your black jeans and zebra-print shoes,
a bunch of anemones in your left hand; your right
reaches mine as I lean from the train.
You hug me as I spill from the journey.
Our mouths touch, we say nothing out loud.
Now, I step back, look at you
properly, my tears wet
on your cheek.
                Our talk on the brief walk home
is of the airplane food, the shop that's shut down,
a politeness that comes of distance,
knowing we'll talk and talk over the next few hours,
days and months, and before morning, we'll be naked –
then time and the longing will stop,
not just in this act but the moving towards
each other, in understanding each other's lives
again. And I will learn to give up
the sadness, the joy and the normality
of having been alone –
and not be reluctant.

Kerry Hardie

THE INADEQUACY OF LETTERS OF CONDOLENCE
 – for a Frenchwoman, living in Ireland

The paper white, the ink black,
your sister, dead in France,
this morning dull with January sloth.

A blackbird in the ruins of the dead perennials,
tossing the sodden leaves,
hunting the worm in the ground.

The thorn hedge, empty and thin, the sheep
moving about in the beet field.
The undramatic January light.

Your wartime childhood.
Your sister in your wartime childhood.
The passionate lost children of our long-dead childhoods.

The whiteness of paper, the blackness of ink.
The link in the chain that's wrenched open;
your link falling loose.

The blackbird rooting as I write this letter.
The sheep in the ravaged beet field
that smells now of fish and decay.

Jean O'Brien

ONCE I WOKE

> Even now there are places where a thought might grow ...
> – Derek Mahon

in a bed on the other side of the world to a waterfall
of light. As sleep cleared from my eyes I recognised
a sheer wall of net curtains transformed
by sunlight, knew then I was in a larger space
than ever before; as if some sextant in my head
had shot the sun, worked out the angle and height of light,
moon and stars, divined that I was far from home.

I tumbled from bed, steadied myself, stood upright
in this new upended world. I checked to see if the water
in the basin curled Coriolis clockwise, a myth of water.
Water memory can hold for hours and then swirl away
withershins as you try to determine drain spin
and trace earth's rotation and wonder if you had
ingested Devil's Berries or Psilocybin.

How we cling to what we know and resist boldly going.
The novelty of umber earth burnished in light and tar roads
that stretch out and out waiting for us to write our story.
Blacktops open to the wide sky, low scrub and miles of bush
beyond the firebreak offer some perspective. At home dirt roads
wend their way up hill and down hemmed in by low stone walls
or cliffs or sight of sea and the lariat line of guide-rope horizon.

This is a place where a thought might grow though racked
by drought with the northern hemisphere reduced to a mere echo.

Nessa O'Mahony

MAP-MAKERS AND TRAVELLERS

Damian Smyth, *English Street* (Templar Poetry, 2018), €12 / £10.
Theodore Deppe, *Liminal Blue* (Arlen House, 2016), €15.
Anne Haverty, *A Break in the Journey* (New Island Books, 2018), €13.95.

In the poem 'Epic', Patrick Kavanagh famously reminded us of the importance of owning a 'half a rood of rock'. His determination to chart 'every blooming thing' of his native Monaghan has been a model for many poets; it's hard to imagine Mayo without thinking of Seán Lysaght or Geraldine Mitchell, or the Beara peninsula without considering Leanne O'Sullivan. Damian Smyth, born and bred in the Lecale district of Co Down, has spent a lifetime capturing every last detail of that territory in seven poetry collections, the most recent of which is *English Street*.

There are 70 poems in this latest collection, and a quick scan through the contents page might suggest both a prevailing interest in local history and a meticulously consistent approach to titling; pretty much every poem title references a place-name, and most titles consist of no more than three or four words including the definite article – 'The Killyleagh Utterances', 'The Bishopscourt Sun Tzu', 'The Minerstown Risen', to name just three (and there are 16 pages of notes at the end to provide historical or literary sources for each poem). Clearly there is more going on here than a random gathering of poems about a specific area. The exactness of the titling is matched by the consistency of the form of each poem: all are one stanza blocks of between 20 and 30 lines. He had a similar experiment in his 2010 collection *Market Street*, where the 70 poems all had uniform long lines; the visual impact here is to create a sense of both substance and method. This book has the mathematical precision of an ordnance survey map.

And if the poems have local subject matter, the quotes that open the collection place them firmly in a wider political context. The first refers to loyalist gunman Michael Stone, the second quotes an 1885 letter from arch-colonialist Rudyard Kipling, describing the 'dark, and crooked and fantastic, and wicked and awe-inspiring life of the "native"'. These quotes set the reader up for poems that explore the life of the native from every angle. No detail is too small for consideration, from the eponymous opening poem 'Tap on English Street', where the tap is 'Like that serpent in the gaol yard in English Street, / Charmed and statuesque for decades, but upright / And swaying if brushed against or in the breeze', to a previously unseen gap in a hedge, as in 'The Ballystrew Routes', where 'even a route you might walk without thinking, is estranged; / Even what remains unmoved, rooted and exactly as it should be, / Is shaken, also, by that disturbance elsewhere, that bearing gone'. Later in the same poem, Smyth states his method clearly:

> … In every single thing, it is about setting out with a purpose,
> So that not only is one travelling the roads, but doing so intently,
> Because they are here for a reason against the camber of the fields

Smyth uses that intent attention to detail to devastating effect in those poems that touch more explicitly on the Troubles. In the poem 'The Bishopscourt Sun Tzu', we are shown in telescopic detail how the art of war was once applied in Northern Ireland (the Chinese warrior Sun Tzu is credited with writing *The Art of War*):

> There remain the options: to walk away, or run;
> Or turn one's face aside; or just stay there,
> As that old man did when they came for his car
> And he refused the keys, not once but several times,
> Even as the muzzle printed between his eyes
> An imperfect 'O', a modest statement of surprise

Elsewhere, there are moments of premonition when a momentary loss foreshadows a permanent one, as in the more personal 'The Teconnaught Cogito', where the disappearance of the poet's friend into a swelling football crowd prefigures his later Troubles-related death and provokes this profound realisation: 'They say that loss is a thing itself, thick like stone / Or light as a call the body makes without reply.' The poem concludes 'The pattern of absence was already known: but not its weight, / Endurance, depth, or how much of it there was.'

For all the tragedy, this is not a gloomy book. There is humour derived from social portraiture in many poems (those masculine presences in the 1970s chip shop in the poem 'The Portofino Conclave', for example), and Smyth constantly reminds us of the importance of small lives, of forgotten histories excavated through memory and the artefacts left behind, as in 'The Coney Island Watchers', where 'fragments / Rise to the surface in any disturbance – broken roof tiles / From a tea house, beams that bore a bridge, shiny tesserae', or in 'The Shambles Trench', where a veteran of World War I 'had on his mantelpiece, / (Speckled and white and blue and brown) / Bone fragments which passed as chalk ornaments'. In the final line of that poem, Smyth calls this 'A mustering, a salute, a funeral he could himself attend', which seems a fair approximation of his own intentions for this masterly collection.

The geographic range of Theodore Deppe's sixth collection is wider than Smyth's (Dresden, the Seine, Venice, Milwaukee), though he too has favoured locations; his beloved north Connemara is the base for a number of poems. The book is divided into three sections: the first made up of 12 poems, the second consists of a lyric essay, and the third is one chapbook-length poem. Many of the poems are autobiographical narratives related in a chatty and sometimes confessional tone; Deppe moves backwards and forwards in time, focussing on events and places with long-held associations.

Memories of the dead are ever-present. The book is dedicated to Deppe's parents, who died in 2009 and 2013, and the long poem that concludes the collection is addressed to the poet's father. Earlier poems allude to other lost influences, such as 'October Postcards from Connemara', with its epigraph from Thomas Tranströmer. In it, the poet writes a series of weather-report postcards to Tranströmer that allow him to play to his strength: the lyric capture of landscape. In the third stanza he records 'Across the bay, / waves strike the cliffs on Caher Island, then hang in the air / ten seconds. Twelve. Fifteen.' The sense of an ongoing dialogue between poets works well here; there's an intimacy of address, rather than any po-faced tribute: 'Force 9: Snot from my nostrils sails a hundred metres over / the bracken. The bellowing of our neighbour's bull flies by.'

The book's second section, 'Memory train', consists of paragraphs of prose poetry in a lyric essay that explores autobiography and what can be remembered. It might be a mission statement for the entire collection:

> This is our first realm, the past, which in its truest state is
> lost to us even if it just happened this morning. So much is
> forgotten and the rest is in fragments, but we're already at
> work valuing this, making a story of that, of remembering,
> which means reinventing, making a moment memorable,
> making it anything but what it was.

The final section, titled 'Little Colloquium by the Sea', takes up the remaining 53 pages of the collection and is broken up into 19 sections of triolets. It is a prolonged meditation on death and loss, starting with an elegy for his parents before moving on to consider other lost friends. The chosen form drives the narrative forward; stylistically it is quite different to the conversational and formal looseness of the earlier poems – for example, from the opening of Section II:

> After a month of conferences
> we arrived home in Ireland
> and my wife led me

into the North Atlantic.
   How could I know
      our hearts wouldn't stop

when we entered those icy
   waters?

The poem works associatively – a mention of a seal in one section brings us to a consideration of Elizabeth Bishop and her poem 'At the Fishhouses' in the next, and onto an exploration of Bishop's childhood home in Nova Scotia in the next again. There's a pleasure in this freewheeling approach, yet we never veer too far from the poem's main source of grief, with dream visions reconnecting the poet to his parents, as in section VIII, with a visit to the Church of the Two Saint Theodores:

    I'd never heard of even one

Saint Theodore, but there in the 14th century
   was a space for my father and myself
     and the door left miraculously

open so I could leave a flame
   for both saints, the sky
     behind them golden, their horses

in perfect harmony.

This is a moving collection, celebrating that liminal space between the living and the dead.

The dedication to Anne Haverty's latest collection reminds us of another deep loss: her husband, Anthony Cronin, died in 2016. Although in the poem 'Forgetting', she argues that 'you can't bring back the dead. / What can they do? / Nothing, only / go on. Forget', the main thrust of the collection is to emphasise the impossibility of forgetting.

The 42 poems here range over entire life cycles, both human and animal. Haverty unites them in her opening poem, 'The Nun and the Greyhound', with its surreal evocation of sister and dog in retirement. A dog's take on grief ('The Dog Will Not Take the Gloom') offers wonderful contrast to an earlier human meditation on the same subject:

If I indulge in despondency or tears,
he who lies constantly at my feet
and leads the way from room to room,

takes himself off
to the neutral area of the stairs.

Perhaps it's because I'm an elderly-dog-owner myself (and only too aware
of the ambiguity of that descriptor), that I was especially moved by the
poems using the old dog as a metaphor for lasting relationships, even
those that outlive death. In 'Stricken While Out Walking With Man and
Dog' we're shown a heart-breaking but hopeful view of eternity. Indulge
me if I quote it in full:

> He
> Is not young
> And dogs
> (they say)
> Do not
> Have souls.
>
> So
> Perfect happiness
> Is not
> To be
>
> Unless I get
> Positive
> Proof
>
> That we three
>
> Will walk again
> In the fields
> of Elyse

There are many physical journeys here, and emotional ones, and much
superb evocation of place. 'Beautiful Day at Birkenau' superbly dissects
how beauty can co-exist with evil, though her final analysis is that it cannot:

> Here
> Is no clemency.
> No clemency
> In humankind.

Haverty is acutely aware of the contradictions of history, and of life. Her
'go on. Forget' is essentially Beckettian in its insistence on the imperative
to survive, despite everything.

Penelope Shuttle

OSTERLEY PARK: SUMMERTIDE TREES
     – for John Greening

lime trees in flower   they make you cups of holy tea
the Oriental plane   *Planatus orientalis*
shuffling along on its many three hundred year old elbows

under such a tree sat Hippocrates   teaching medicine in its shade

in our deckchairs we are tiny   only trees are big at Osterley
green wolf-lords   leaf-thanes ruling over crows and parakeets
here's the genial Cork Oak   an official Great Tree of London

venerable *Quercus suber*   *a real corker* says local press
Cedars-of-Lebanon   needling the sky   death-defying yews
that plane tree still wriggling along the North Lawn

oxen joy of summer   is what the Osterley trees know
rain-humming   to the bees buzzing the big shot's garden
still gossiping about Lady Child after all these years

Author's Note: The magnificent Georgian mansion, Osterley
Park, in Middlesex, was built originally for Thomas Gresham.
It was remodelled by Robert Adam for Robert Child, grandson
of Sir Francis Child, founder of the Child's Bank. Robert Child's
daughter, Sarah Anne Child (Lady Child), eloped with the rakish
Earl of Westmoreland.

Quinlan Corbett

DA CAPO

I wish I could hear god in the shapes
as my brother can.

Above me Snow Geese agglomerate
and disperse.

Small flanks of blue clouds puff their chests
then vanish.

The aperture of evening narrows,
while the continuo

casts its net through the grid of time
on which the geometries

shimmer – it's like listening to math
while the sky sings.

Paul Jeffcutt

IRON ANNIVERSARY

Old Cantley wakes to cries
stabs scrawny long-johned legs
into shit-stained old suit trousers
held at the waist with baler twine
drags on hobnailed boots
frayed flannel shirt and once-green jersey
smeared with dregs from countless feeds
scrapes a greasy cap onto a grizzled head
kicks open the door to the stinking yard.
Rooks scatter and caw above the sycamore
his chained collie bitch stretches and yawns
filthy water dribbles over battered concrete
oozing between clods and spilled hay
as bullocks roar and clatter in the corrugated barn.

Hunching against the sleet that spears from Blue Hill
he slings the mildewed heel of a loaf at the collie
she snatches it from the muck and gulps it whole
pads close and licks his hand. He howls
clamps his great gnarled paws around her neck
heaves the collie into the air
her frantic legs tearing against him
forces scarred thumbs into warm matted fur
squeezing her whining white throat
ever tighter
to stop the screams
of his young wife and wean
tearing down the rickety stairs
and away.

Ray Malone

NOT TO KNOW

you were not to know   not to see
the hand in front of your eyes
the forbidding finger raised
you were not to find the words
before your time
not to be told when the time was
or would be   ever be

you were to be still   to be
the silent one in the corner there
a credit to your own account
to your name
you were to stand there
staring at life
ashamed

a stranger to the way fared
to the words heard

you were not to hear   to feel
the earth under your feet
the stir of the worms at work
you were not to fear
to fall
not to call out   cry
for help   raise a single doubt

you were to be you   you
who saw the hand there   felt
the finger raised   heard
all the words   found your time
saw all that stirred   you
who knew
you were not to know

Susan Wicks

AFTER A DAUGHTER'S MISCARRIAGE

Cove Park, September 2016

If you wake early to leave home
while it's still dark, driving or being driven
along a winding road
where trees reach out and touch
and magpies – three of them, I counted –
hop and flutter on the tarmac,
and you're travelling by car and then by plane
through cloud to land in Glasgow, then by bus
where at an unexpected bend your case
decides to leave you on its own four wheels,
and then in stops and starts
by train to Gourock, where there's a sudden
rainbow so low-slung it almost lies
on the horizon, more a bow
and less an arch than any you have seen
and mirrored in the water –
then by boat that dips and bobs and sways
towards Kilgerran, finally
by pick-up here, where wind and rain
across the surface of a pond
swirl endlessly like someone blowing
on a bowl of soup
beyond the time of cooling, far beyond
the time of thirst or hunger
till the mouth that blew
has surely died and yet it still goes on
in silver, black, a sweeping cloud
of rain that dances forward, back,
a quick-step on the surface –

Then you tell yourself that no one really
knows that what is dead
is truly dead, or only practising
the way this rain, this quick-quick forward-back
retreats, collects itself, and hesitates,
prepares to come again.

Traci Brimhall

WHY I STAYED

Because the mirror rose over the night garden, melancholy
and bronze. Because I greeted the moon wearing eyeshadow

green as a scarab and nothing else. Because like Artemis
I fed a man to his hounds. Because all summer I wanted

to die but chose not to trust my feelings. Instead, I took 99
of the peacock's eyes, half the checking account, and left.

Because I watched spokes of light sow my animus into
a flock of shadows. Because when I catalogued gratitudes

I listed high thread counts, gin and tonics, bedrooms with
skylights, jeans on sale and how good my ass looked in them.

Because cabbage-white butterflies in the buttercups and
sea salted caramels never failed to gladden me. Because

I hoped to die painlessly, like a star. Because young sheep
needed their backs tarred to ward off foxes and crows.

Because like Psyche I was careless with candles. Because joy
returned with a kiss crisp as a dried bee that became a stab

of honey on my tongue. Because I wanted to love someone
who wouldn't count my sobs as proof. Because I found

a thousand small pleasures that made me want to live, and
they were bridges, birdsong, strawberries, sunlight and lambs.

Maria Johnston

SOMETHING ELSE

Nick Laird, *Feel Free* (Faber and Faber, 2018), £14.99.
Ciaran Carson, *From There to Here: Selected Poems and Translations* (The Gallery Press, 2018), €13.90.

> Like some son looking for his father, or the father for his son,
> We try to piece together the exploded fragments.
>> – CIARAN CARSON, 'HAMLET', *Belfast Confetti* (1989)

In his most accomplished poetry collection to date, Nick Laird takes on the complex topics of parenthood and parentage as he moves through a world that is in chaotic spin. As well as being an intensely elegiac naviga-tion of 'sensational loss' both politically and personally – his mother's death is the drifting emotional core of the collection – *Feel Free* forms a vibrant sounding space of poetic inheritance. Paul Muldoon dedicated *New Weather* to his 'Fathers and Mothers' and, in *Feel Free*, Laird's debt to poetic parents such as Muldoon, John Ashbery, Elizabeth Bishop, and Sylvia Plath is felt. But it seems to me that Laird is also in dialogue with another Northern Irish poet, Ciaran Carson, throughout, signalled through his engagement with Shakespeare's *Hamlet* which is, for Carson, 'a play about fathers and sons and the ghosts they have to exorcise [...] a discussion of the morality of violence and terrorism', and crucially, one might add, a play that exists in multiple versions. Like Carson's, Laird's poetry is fiercely syncopated: the state and time we live in being 'out of joint'. 'In America you're just free to imagine that you're free', Carson once commented, and the pressing reality of the poetic imagination both energises and exacerbates *Feel Free* as Laird, poet out of Tyrone now resi-dent in the USA, questions what it means to live both in and out of this world and between worlds, as metaphysics and quantum physics merge in wild interplay and staggering questions to do with freedom and con-tainment hurtle across disorienting linguistic registers – the poet himself vaulting between formal necessity and free verse, between textual and bodily, online and off-line, versions of the self.

All begins with a glitch, that is, a poem titled 'Glitch'. Meaning a 'disturbance or malfunction', it can also, in its slippery way, suggest, 'a sudden surge of current or spurious electronic signal' (*OED*). The poem opens in freefall as mind takes leave of body and time itself splits: 'More than ample, a deadfall of one metre eighty / to split my temple apart on the herringbone parquet, / and crash the OS, tripping an automated shutdown', and ends with 'all // particulars of my other life fled except the sense / that lasts for hours of being wanted somewhere else'. This stunning opener is one of the keys to the collection, with that word *herringbone* underlining the obliquity of what is to come just as the closing destination of *somewhere else* opens up the dizzying momentum of transport across space and time that gives this collection its stretch and pull. It is, moreover, a sonnet, both time-bound and timeless, and part of that great tradition of terrifying contemporary sonnets that includes Muldoon's 'Why Brownlee Left' and Ashbery's 'At North Farm'. There is not one poem in this entire collection that is content to stay put or exist in one-dimensional fashion. The challenge and delight for the reader is to keep up.

Formally, Laird is on fire throughout. In 'Parenthesis', a pantoum, the poet and his sleeping family are reconfigured as punctuation marks and typographical symbols – chillingly reminiscent of Carson's 'Belfast Confetti' from *The Irish For No* (1987) which opens: 'Suddenly as the riot squad moved in it was raining exclamation marks', and asks: 'Why can't I escape? Every move is punctuated.' Laird has prior history with the pantoum in a way that similarly forces art and life into bed together. In her 2005 novel *On Beauty*, Zadie Smith (Laird's wife) has a character present Laird's 'On Beauty' as an example of a 'broken pantoum', a Malay form that (significantly, like the poet himself) 'has travelled'. With its pattern of repeated interlocking lines, the pantoum is one of the forms that, according to Ashbery, 'occupy the conscious mind to the extent that the unconscious is liberated and can go about the business of contributing to the poem'. Despite its constraints it is a form that could keep on going, recalibrating itself, refusing closure, much like 'Silk Cut', a poem about his father in widowhood, which cannot bring itself to come to a full stop or continue to form the expected sonnet:

> and we are going home, waiting
> at the turn for the traffic, when I find
> I have to stop my hand from taking his

Negotiating such existential twists and turns, the poet himself is a figure cut-off, involved in the business of cuts and (un)folds as patterns emerge alongside random disorder. Crepuscular, 'The Folding' opens 'In the midst of this lifelike grief' yet, despite its calm, crystalline exterior of deftly patterned sonnets, it reveals poetic form as embodying agonising emotional experience not as something imposed on words or extraneous to meaning: 'and the held breath / as the kids concentrate on symmetries / or the blades' irresistible path'. The way these sinuous seven-line stanzas expand and contract concertina-like leaves the reader gasping for breath. The figure of Hamlet looms large and with that the crushing burden of guilt; the poetic persona as the son who coldly 'takes out a pad and a quill to begin / getting it down in all its squalid detail' ('The Good Son', i). What does it mean to live in the apprehendable world and to constantly work living beings into textual form? The high-octane 'The Vehicle and The Tenor' hurtles towards a clenching final address to you, the poet's dead mother, who 'kept on lying in here, past all metaphor, / / left by yourself on the cleared stage like a real corpse'. The poet's gaze is unflinching. Fathers and sons, unseeing, are all fair game for art:

> And I like when I give you the nightfeed, Harvey, how you're
> concentrating on it: fists clenched, eyes shut, like this *is* bliss.
>
> – 'FEEL FREE'

Whether by accident or design, this brings us back to the closing image of 'Cuttings' – the opening poem of Laird's debut *To A Fault* (2005) – wherein we find the father's 'eyes budded shut'. Indeed, the spill-over lines of 'Feel Free' come to a close with the poet imaginatively feeling his way home: 'I like to lie here / with my eyes closed and think about my schoolfriends' houses before / choosing one to walk through slowly, room by sunlit room'. If the 'sunlit absence' of Heaney's 'Mossbawn: Sunlight' with its insistent 'now' is invoked here, the poet Laird is in more than two places at once, momentarily achieving the 'neutral buoyancy' that he desires.

As one thing leads to another, mention of Nina Simone's 'The Twelfth of Never' in 'Feel Free' reminded me of an account of Simone in performance from Smith's 2016 novel *Swing Time*:

> I thought of her voice, the way she could extend a note beyond the point
> of tolerability and force her audience to concede to it, to her timescale,
> to her vision of the song, how she was completely without pity for her
> audience, and so relentless in pursuit of her freedom!

This, to me, perfectly describes the atmosphere of *Feel Free* and Laird's ability to compose poems as incantations, as trance-like states that haunt the ear and that we cannot leave lightly behind. At times I had to stop to come up for air, such is the pressure being exerted. Perhaps it is in art only that we can achieve a discontinuous freedom. If this book gives joy it is 'joy' as defined by Smith in an essay of that title from her 2018 essay collection *Feel Free*: 'that strange admixture of terror, pain and delight that I have come to recognise as joy, and now must find some way to live with daily'. This is a hard-hitting, breathtaking collection that leaves one winded and bewildered.

In serendipitous fashion, Simone's 'The Twelfth of Never' brings us to the 1998 collection of the same name by Carson, about which he has commented: 'The book, is basically the underworld, the otherworld, the in-between world that is not ostensibly the real world. Because behind this "apparition" of the real world there is a lot more going on than we know.' Laird and Carson hold much in common, not least it seems to me the idea of writing itself as, to quote Carson again, 'an alternative universe' central to which is the form or spirit of the aisling as 'an interlingual twilight zone'. Self-described as one who 'likes to go walking in hyperspace', Carson is a massive poet who understands art as a process of infinite variation and who makes language(s) perform impossible feats of movement as he manipulates the fabric of space-time. As the poet of Belfast his Belfast poems, as Alan Gillis has observed, 'work to cast the reader into a dynamically unsettled, vividly rendered, perpetually shifting world'. Like Laird in 'Feel Free', Carson is similarly 'taken with the possibilities / of radical formal shifts and tonal ambiguities' and, as with Laird, the reader does not get away lightly.

Embarking on his new *Selected Poems and Translations* I wondered how such an edited selection could honour the sense of structural sequence that is to integral to Carson's individual collections, from *Belfast Confetti* (1989) to *For All We Know* (2008) and *On the Night Watch* (2009). Then I looked more closely. In fact, in this new *Selected*, Carson, he of infinite playfulness, has changed the order of poems within each collection. 'Don't get too comfortable', this most profoundly unsettling of poets seems to warn the reader. I'm going to go out on a limb here and suggest that this poem from *Until Before After* (2010) tells you all you need to know about Carson's methods here and elsewhere:

> *It's the same*
>
> old story
> but not
>
> as we know
> it we thought
>
> it was
> a box
>
> until we found
> the key on
>
> the verge of
> these words

Just look at what he's doing here with the line breaks. Every crossing from one word to another and then across the line, the stanza, the silence, requires sustained attention. Much as Ginsberg said of William Carlos Williams' line-brinkmanship, it's as though language and perception have been washed clean. Every multi-faceted word gleams and announces itself, refreshed. The poems are mobile arrangements intent on escaping the eye, fleeing as they appear.

Whether teasing out long lines to the limits of pliability or paring back the poetic line to a precision-cut fragility, Carson's great gift is to reveal the mind as it moves and processes elusive experience – he has, after all, defined translation as 'to move something from one place to another' – and admits the fictiveness of our deepest-held certainties: time, history, language, and memory. Before Anna Burns's *Milkman* we had Carson's disquieting narrators weaving their vertiginous stories, destabilising official narratives, turning 'truth' on its head, and, thanks to his own hyphenated existence between languages, 'deeply suspicious of language in general' (as Carson has described himself). This new presentation of the poems highlights Carson not merely as a translator but as a translator of translations and as a poet who, like Emily Dickinson, continues to dwell in unending possibility (incidentally, his 'Planxty Miss Dickinson' makes the cut).

What comes into sharper focus throughout is Carson's own parentage in poems that hinge on his father as mapper and storyteller and, beyond Belfast, that open out onto the shimmering hypertextuality of his work. This book seems bottomless. No reading of a Carson poem is the same. Fittingly, 'Translation' (from 2014's *From Elsewhere*) ends with a boy who has returned to his house: 'its occupants / addressing him / as if he had not been / changed in the meantime / that is elsewhere'. Despite the insouciant invitation to the reader at the book's head – aistrigh liom siar sa ród / journey back with me along the road – there is no journeying back. With every turn, 'history is changed' ('Turn Again').

Maureen Boyle

THE NUNWELL LETTER

Written at Nunwell House, Brading, The Isle of Wight, April 1612

John

It has been an untenably long winter
and our baby died.

There, I have told you,
though you may have heard in other ways by now.
This ends my islanded silence
just as spring comes in.
I had not thought to keep it
out of any spite but
I have been more of body John,
than soul, one of those you felt inferior,
sub-lunary, that thin airy chain
made heavy and lowered,
brought to earth by loss.

I wonder where you are now?
It is almost impossible for letters to go from here
or for them to reach us for fear of France
but my brother came at Christmas and said
you hearkened for news
full of illness and worry.

I could not write earlier
and I wanted to be the one to tell you.

I know you feel that letters link souls,
let this be a mending link in ours.

2.
Our first weeks here in your absence
were good though the children missed you.

It was a mild autumn and they could be in the fields
in the day and help in the farmyard.
They collected the mast of the beech trees

to feed to the pigs in their darkened byres
and the little ones especially loved to be lifted up
to gaze into the rank, rich space, Lucy's eyes lightening
in awe at the sow lolling in the mud.

Frances is up each day with the dew to help
in cleaning out the stalls and often ours troop
out into the dawn after her to help or hinder
before the full household is awake.

It is a different life John and their uncle
is a different kind of father.
He is a good man
and my sister loves him
but he is dull, as is the life here.

I miss the wit of your writing and your speech,
our little house at Mitcham with its own smells
and our bed.

3.
The day we came to the island the sea on the Solent was flat,
the cliffs a mirage before us, the children entranced.

There is a staircase in the house
that delights them and me.
It rises like three branches of the vast tree it was hewn from
and makes the house feel simultaneously light and weighted.
From underneath, it looks like the rigging of a great ship
and going to bed we joke that we are climbing the mainsail,
George and Francis playing pirates on its steps and newel posts.

I have a little room where each night one of the older children
slept beside me until my confinement when I was too unwell.

4.
When we arrived, the children saw the Oglander crest everywhere
and it seemed like a good omen – the stork – and I told them
of the storks you had seen on the chimney pots of Strasbourg,
their nests top-heavy and chaotic, as if they'd topple the house.

Remember how I had so wanted to go with you that time too
and you teased me with telling me that as a woman
I would be lusted after in France and as a disguised page
the same in Italy for a man!

This has been the hardest parting John
even as I understand its necessity.

The first time – when my father brought me back to Loseley
from my uncle and aunt's house, not knowing we were married,
there was the thrill of holding that secret in me,

and the second time there was a sense of novelty mixed with fear
since I would be taken to bed with George alone
but all was well and I liked the time to myself again
a line break or lacuna in a poem.

But now this is hard
even with our children here,
it is only a half-life without you.

5.
When the baby came, I had a midwife who lives
a rose-rent tenant on the farm and has delivered
all of Frances's babies. It was a cold night
and they lit a fire for me in the room
and the children stayed until I was in too much pain
and then the little one was born.

She was perfect John, but didn't breathe.
The woman told me in the old faith she'd
have gone to the *limbus infantum* – the very hem of hell –
and as she washed her I swear she used the water drops
to commend her soul to God.
I wonder where her soul goes then?
I hope to heaven and to Him.

They took her to Brading to bury her the next day
in an Oglander grave. I was too sick to go
but I have been since and planted it
with hellebore and winter aconite
for the season when she came. It is a little plot
by the sea-wall of St Mary-the-Virgin, where every day
she is by sea-spray newly christened.

I called her Agnes for the saint whose day it was
in the old calendar and because
the midwife covered me in the skin
of one of Oglander's sheep to help me heal
along with bay-leaves, rupture-wort and chamomile
that she'd smear as lovingly as you on my poor torn body.

I worry that we will leave her here so far from us
but pray my soul and hers can endure just such
an expansion as you imagined.

6.

During the baby's birth
I found that place I've told you of
in my other labours where time stops
and I'm contracted into myself
even as the body convulses.

I was a child again in grandfather's library
surrounded by his beloved books
sitting in a puddle of sun by the tall windows
in a different kind of abstraction.

In the worst pain,
almost as if knowing what I faced,
I was Niobe turned to stone in grief
or Rhea, smeared with the soilure of birth,
her after-blood seeping into a dry river bed,
commanding the earth mother to create
a new stream to clean her and her god-child.

And then it was as if I had two souls
and two sets of eyes,
those of the child, for whom this was all story
and those of the woman
whose cold child is placed in her arms –
a still, ever-sleeping girl
who I will never know.

And in the moment of seeing her –
it is hard to say this but –
I wanted to follow her John
and thought of your *Biathanatos*

but knew that God would not forgive my leaving
our other children.

And in the days of fever afterwards I was betimes
in our waking days of first glances at dinner
the thrill of passing one another close in busy corridors,
first words, the hours of fascinated talk
and then nights it seemed we hardly needed sleep
and the quickening sense that I had found my life.

7.
My reclusion was like the season
full of tears but by necessity hidden from the children.
I found refuge in the still room
making medicines for the house
while winter rain beat against its windows
and winds whistled under its rafters.

You cannot mourn one child too long
when there are others to care for
and so it is spring and I am looking to return.

This must be the longest time my body has had to rest
since we met – neither nursing nor pregnant.

Come home when you can and we will begin again.

Ann

Author's Note: This poem was written as a commission from the inaugural Ireland Chair of Poetry Travel Bursary, which I was awarded in 2017. The award allowed me to travel to the Isle of Wight where John Donne's wife Ann spent the winter of 1611 and the spring of 1612, while Donne travelled to Europe with Robert Drury and his wife. Ann lost a child during this absence, and I wanted to attempt to give her a voice partly in response to Donne's 'Valediction Forbidding Mourning', the poem he gave her by way of consolation on leaving, and partly because she's a silent presence known only from his love poems. For information about the Ireland Chair of Poetry Travel Bursary, e-mail **irelandchairofpoetry@gmail.com**

Amy Nocton

BITTERSWEET LAPIS

There will be blueberries
staining skin
bittersweet lapis,
and stone tile,
smooth and silent,
underfoot,
shaded lunches terraced,
and umbrellas,
lightly clanking like boats moored lazily,
seduced by the sea breeze,
azure.

There will be moody skies,
rain-washed lips,
and landlocked lakes,
sheltered by mountains dotted violet
and marigold yellow
memories.

There will be surf,
salt skin, bones ache,
stinging, cold chased
by ocean-eyed tea,
and stolen glances in mirrors, tapestries
unweaving.

Alison Jones

EILEEN

She went before I had time to really know her,
down-sized, not always visible behind the dashboard.
Thin in grey mornings, yet cloaking us all in hard work,
northern grit. Service at fifteen on bended knee,
Brasso and donkey stones. The Family.
The daily grind of polishing and perfecting, done
before rest had risen, with no idea of what was involved.

I had no idea of what was involved. Before the rest have risen,
lines turned between pages in different spaces. Again,
a daily grind on bended knee, family; an absence
of Brasso and donkey stones. Hard work cloaking us still in northern grit.
In thin grey mornings, up-scaled, head above the parapet,
how I'd love to have her drive me through the years.
She went before I had time to really know her.

Róisín Sheehy

OIRÍON

Luite ar burlaí tuí
Dúiris: "níl aon radharc chomh breá
Le hoíche ghealaí i Pontrhydfendigaid"

D'fhigheas mo mhéaranta tríd do ghruaig
D'fháisceas d'fholt i mo dhorn
Bhí greim againn ar na réaltbhuíonta

ORION

Lying on haybales
You said: "There's no view as mighty as a
Starry night at Pontrhydfendigaid"

I wove my fingers through your hair
Squeezed your locks in my fist
We held the constellations

– translated by **Róisín Sheehy**

Martin Malone

THIS GLITTERING WORLD

Anna Woodford, *Changing Room* (Salt Publishing, 2018), £9.99.
Ailbhe Darcy, *Insistence* (Bloodaxe Books, 2018), £9.95.
Virginia Astley, *The English River* (Bloodaxe Books, 2018), £12.

A debut and two second collections brimming with fine poetry and qualities
distinct to each of the three poets under scrutiny, these were a genuine
pleasure to read. The sophomore efforts of Woodford and Darcy are
linked, superficially at least, by the theme of first motherhood, though
each raise sons to the tune of its own lucid music. Anna Woodford's
Changing Room opens eponymously with a short sequence on this very
theme, in which her artfully spare verse quickly registers the strengths
that most distinguish this collection. There are clear sightlines to this
poetry, which are harder to achieve than one might assume, and which
headily evoke that reawakened sense of vivid childhood so often gifted
to parenthood. Poems like 'Mother and Mother and Child' and 'What
Archie Gets' convincingly evoke the metamorphic nature of motherhood
with just the right dash of surreal detail, fantasy, and poignancy: 'A mother
hiding // in the nursery office, practising / being miles away' ('What
Archie Gets). Likewise, 'School Run' and 'Journey' – the latter describes
how 'we had crawled away from the maw of the hospital / entrance' to a
world transformed by its new fact:

> Town was out of reach as scissors; gated like the stairs
> in my safe house which overnight had become
> an evangelical church in an ordinary-looking terrace
> devoted to the cult of you.

Motherhood is a theme unavoidably common to much poetry written in
this or any era, but it is difficult to do as well as this and with such conviction of its own individuality. These are qualities common to both Woodford and Darcy, who use it as a central thread to their collections but
also get beyond its all-embracing reality to showcase far greater thematic
range. In Woodford's case, the clarity of her line is melded to
an impressive technical control and freshness of seeing that yields a run
of fine 'parent' poems like 'Late Journey with my Father' (one of a few
'meta' poems that artfully self-signals), 'In Passing', and 'Portrait of
Dorothy Hodgkin as my Mother with a Broken Hip'. Other domestic
concerns – such as marriage breakdown and the day job – are redolent
with a characteristic lightness of touch, as is the theme of memory in

an ekphrastic poem like 'Shrine', wherein Woodford displays an acute instinct for poems' beginnings and endings to achieve a quirky sense of perspective, and the transcendental nature of living memory is instigated by the innate shortcomings of a photograph. A poem like 'The walls are only there because you impute them' is a brilliantly allusive poem that playfully eludes meaning, yet chimes with its own felt logic. Overall, this was a collection worthy of the praise on its own back cover.

Ailbhe Darcy's *Insistence* was shortlisted for the TS Eliot Prize, and clearly transcends all need of my approval but, for what it's worth, this is a collection hopping with its own word-jazz. At its best, the poetry is improvisational, inventive, and headily convincing in its bid to sweep the reader along with its insistent energy. In a poem like 'Still', there is a fascinating use of language and phrasing that, at times, seems to recreate the skittish nature of thought itself:

> Some things are unnameable—
> or some names are unspeakable— but we
> are well capable of words—

Similarly, the book's opener, 'Ansel Adams' Aspens' is an intriguing 'mixed-media' meditation upon the 'isness' of artistic inspiration, enacted by its own language and skilfully-managed effects to intimate an imagined screenplay: 'To tiny Ansel Adams, newly arrived on this earth, / the sky is what it is, taut with its isness.' Tight control offsetting structural ingenuity becomes a distinguishing feature of the book throughout, and serves it well, particularly in the longer sequential poems, such as 'Postcards from Europe' and, ultimately, the abecedarian that is the collection's 'Wreck of the Deutschland'. Impressive of form but risking a sense of *Insistence* trailing off into mere exercise, 'Alphabet' works because of Darcy's nerve and formal authority footing the high-wire of inventiveness seen in earlier poems. This allows the longer piece to burst in on its own moments of vivid life and provides it with a sort of *haecceitas*-driven underpinning, particularly in the ninth poem of the sequence, apparently about her young son and boasting some lovely turns-of-phrase:

> Icarus in that split second
> before the fall still as a hatchet fish;
> Icarus high as a kite, blank with the no-going-back of it;
> this being his one interval of lambency
> between blank and blank …

As with *Changing Room*, the subject of motherhood yields some of the book's most memorable moments, though the treatment tends to be more vividly impressionistic and visceral, as in the two poems called 'After my son was born', which frankly evoke the downright uncomfortable nature of parenthood at times:

> I'd a snip cut in his tongue.
> Blood scissored down his chin.
> At every squall I'd be unsnibbing
> myself and starving him. He knocked
> me so my nose coughed blood ...

However, what distinguishes this collection again and again is the always fascinating journeys you are encouraged to take in each poem, as a result of its wonderful balance of control with feverish linguistic invention. The paean to female corporeality in 'Hair', the skewed description of the American interlude where this collection was begun, in 'A guided tour of the house and its environs', and the jazzy riffing of 'Silver' and 'Mushrooms' which presage the 'Alphabet' sequence: all showcase the idiosyncratic qualities of Darcy's craft. Often, as in 'Angelus', she offers us just the cumulative charge of words to create a resonant aggregate effect which retains a sense of the poem's instinctive level of 'meaning', without fretting overmuch about that as an end in itself. It takes a confident poet, bold of purpose and in full command of her methods, to carry this off.

To readers of a certain vintage, Virginia Astley's eminence in the 'pastoral pop' rack of the independent music store of the 1980s might yet be familiar. I first encountered her in 1981 as headline member of The Ravishing Beauties, then supporting The Teardrop Explodes at Liverpool's legendary Club Zoo; and recall her winsomely groomed image staring back at me from the vinyl collection of many a good friend. An unusual hinterland from which to set out, then, and one which many a debut poet might struggle to match with current practice. Fortunately, time and talent have been more than kind to Astley, who has produced, here, a deeply impressive and hugely rewarding first collection.

The English River flows elegantly around its central subject – the Thames – beginning at its source in Gloucestershire and running through Wiltshire, Oxfordshire, Berkshire, Surrey and on towards its final sequence in the nation's capital. Astley takes us on a meditative journey down this most iconic of rivers and, in doing so, evokes a landscape already highly scrutinised and freighted with cultural resonance. That she manages this while maintaining the sense of a distinctive and strong poetic identity of her own is, perhaps Astley's greatest achievement, here. Starting, appropriately enough, with the impressionistic details and form of 'Source', *The English River* meanders memorably through what might be described as *L'Angleterre Profonde*, each poem discretely complemented by the accompanying verso images, supplied by the poet herself. This discretion – a kitemark of the book as a whole – is important, since the verse, itself, more than carries the collection.

What I find most impressive is the discrimination and restraint of Astley's quiet lyricism: nowhere does she overstay or overdo her sharp-eyed and clearly felt descriptions of the river; rarely does she succumb to mythologising either her own past or the river's significance beyond the ghost-wracked moments conjured by its course through a heartland. Yet there is always just enough descriptive detail to betray an intimacy with the landscape while making capital of the book's organising principle of the river journey. The early course of 'Lammas Land' hints at the poet's closeness to her subject, with its nod to the river's geology and flora; in 'Sanctuary', away across the meadow, Oxford's 'skyline of spires' lies distant as *Jude*; and the poet's musical past creeps in with 'The white noise flanged / and phased' of 'The Weir at Benson'.

One is aware of the vari-distant touch points of this landscape with the poet's own course, as she visits or revisits moments in the company of ghosts and past selves, often registered by the discrete lyricism of tense and pronoun. We become aware of a fluid state of aloneness or company, often only late in the poem; such as in 'Kelmscott', where the 'We' that eases the reader into place is suddenly particularised in the final line: 'and you stand by the stream smiling, your / newly-washed hair caught in the flare of May'. The overall effect is, as I say, one of discrete lyricism and an intimacy that flows into and out of the more vivid landscape descriptions, such as in the poem 'Sometimes, in this glittering world', where, lost under the stress of an old idea:

> I focus on
> small things: thatch dripping, snowdrops
> pushing through, how to split the logs,
> but caught by a memory of unlit windows
> and a wanting, I go back to that year
> and the woods

There are obvious contemporary parallels between this book and the Alice Oswald of *Dart*. However, the chief presiding spirits of *The English River* are those of Thomas Hardy and Edward Thomas. The former is, perhaps, to be expected, given that Astley has, in effect, been the ghostly Tom's charwoman at Max Gate these past few years. Certainly, in the book's central sequence, with poems like 'Whitehill', 'Old Songs', and 'Sometimes, in this glittering world', there is a sensibility reminiscent of *Poems 1912-13*. However, the latter is also materially present, both in spirit and in the quiet technical innovation Thomas introduced to the English line. A good example of this is the badger poem, 'Coleshill in February', in which the subject is buried within the poem's winter landscape and is only revealed by the hypozeugma of the last line's naming, a feature that recalls a poem like 'Roads':

> Even before the sun was up
> the day had folded in
>
> the field and houses subdued
> below the night's snow
>
> the alley from yard to lane
> deep with drifts   and still
>
> only a single track gave evidence
> of her cold journey
>
> the five-round-toe-and-kidney
> shaped pads or her paws
>
> imprinted in the sticking flakes
> as badger made her way   searching

Ultimately, then, *The English River* is remarkable for its convincing reinvigoration of an English pastoral tradition, once more 'worn new'.

Andrea Potos

BRACING MYSELF

Another morning choosing the seasonal
dark dress, the dark purse to match, again
the hour drive to the town of my childhood
in time for the vast hour called visitation,
handshaking and embracing, weight
of salt in gilded air, the long chanting,
smoke from the censors expanding and dispersing,
then the flagged trail of slow cars, the opened ground,
sprawl of roses left behind, loss settling
into our bodies like sediment, fatigue deepening
even as relief begins to rise and we make our way
toward the country club or restaurant, to be sated with
grilled fish or steak, Greek potatoes and conversation
and the blessed glasses of wine.

Ben Bransfield

OCTOBER

Housemaster and boarders have gone home.
The gravel drive has let loose its stubble
and the pond is up to the sedge, the rugby boot.

The monument on Lilleshall Hill
wet, even from here, as the hoover
behind in Longford Hall sucks the life
out of the carpet, rattles down a toenail.

Everybody's pagan for a week.
Chimney after chimney offers up
its conclave for the Witch King to read.

Anita Gracey

A SOCIAL WORKER, A HOME-HELP AND A GP WALK INTO A SERVICE USER'S LIFE

During the home visit
the client presents herself as capable but has fatigue
she wants a home-help to clean
but there is no budget for cleaners
I'm a social worker not a miracle worker!
I'll get her a cook.
She became argumentative saying
it will take away her skills
getting her a cook would disable her more.
It's beyond my control
I'm here to facilitate.

The travel time don't talk to me – beam me up Sadie!
I'm not paid for this!
Madam put them organic carrots on her shopping list
they're awful expensive so I got her normal carrots,
thinking of her purse
oh did she give me grief!
Said I'd taken another decision away from her.
It's beyond my control
I'm phoning in sick the-morra.

She says she feels institutionalised in her own home
eating food which isn't her choice
at times of day which suit home-helps' workload.
Institutional living is people in hospitals or care homes
she doesn't comprehend she's actually very lucky
patients who acquire impairments have a loss of control
this has manifested in her non-compliance
and occasional aggression.
It's beyond my control
I'll prescribe a short course of Temazepam.
That'll do the trick.

Emma Must

TO THE PUMP HOUSE

I wanted what was massive: pipes and turbines, engines, rigs and docks.
And water, gallons of it, whooshing out, pushing to make everything clean again.

The heavens promised rain. The God of Machinery sent grabbing claws and a
    pilot boat.
Something heavy was being loaded or off-loaded; several cranes began to swivel.

I wanted water, but what I got instead were terms I didn't understand:
penstock filling valves, impeller blades, the Redfern Kelly Diagram.

The only water to be found here, the only sort not piped in a loop and played
    over-loud
on the walkways before the clanging started, was the stillness of the Lough itself.

Then, skulking in the graving dock, a patina of moss and salty oozes; the clop of
    hooves
resounding from the walls; cardboard cut-outs of inventors wearing bowler hats.

And stacks of keel-blocks with wooden buffers to cushion the hull while it was
    painted,
her rudder and propellers fitted, poles wedged to the side to maintain stability.

Here, without water, something less than monstrous was being finished:
its antonyms, in fact, of good and kind, a guardedness, a reticence to hope.

When I reckon up my losses – two deaths, one friendship, one ill-advised
and half-arsed love, two years, and then two more – what am I left with?

A faint sense of nausea as ripples flicker out towards the sea; the swimming-pool
    blues
and cyans in the Pump House; the white-faced dials of the Piano, gauging the flow.

And, hanging in the clock tower, the Accumulator Block – that concrete counter-
    weight –
its tonnage ready to drop, to inch the caisson gate open, winch in the ships.

Christine Paice

THE STATUE

I was thinking of asking my friend
the late sculptor to create me
out of bronze and place me facing
the setting sun one hand extended
for posterity but then it would look
like I was always beseeching
and I've done enough of that.
I could consider the huge unmoveable
abstract by the fence, the boundary
between who I am and who I want to be
but now I think I'll ask the dead man
to carve me out of stone.

David Hanly

VOICES

I have a disability.

Or am I disabled?

Every day I fight
The voices in my head.

Burden, failure, hopeless,
They scream at me.

Never free from
The voices in my head.

Best foot forward,
Hiding my pain.

Without my disability,
What would I be?

Francis Hesketh

after 'AN IRISH AIRMAN FORESEES HIS DEATH'

   'Some say the devil is dead …'

and buried in Killarney.
The Provos put up a mural saying: *'Our struggle continues …'*
on the Falls Road, right before the turn into the Shankill Road.
Try reading really hard between those lines, my dudes.

   'Some say he rose again …'

and joined the British Army.
The boys on my street were funny, but please, no more pilots.
No, I mean flyers – don't hand them to me when I'm driving down
my road, sorry.

Máirín Nic Eoin

THE STUFF OF WHICH THEY'RE MADE

Peter Fallon and Aifric Mac Aodha (eds.), *Calling Cards: Ten Younger Irish Poets with translations into English* (The Gallery Press and Poetry Ireland/ Éigse Éireann, 2018), €12.50.

I was asked recently if there was a contemporary poetry movement in Irish akin to what has come to be described as the INNTI movement of the late 1960s, 1970s, and 1980s. The question reminded me of conversations over the years about the worrying dearth of young emerging poets in Irish. As the INNTI generation were ageing, concerns were expressed that excitement about poetry among the young, engendered in no small part by that movement's association with counter-cultural politics and activism, had somehow dissipated as Ireland entered the new millennium.

No dedicated poetry publication akin to INNTI can be cited today, yet there is no shortage of periodicals, both Irish-language and dual-language, that welcome new work in Irish. There does not appear to be a geographical cluster or centre of activity for poetry in Irish, but that poetry is seen and heard, published and performed, in a wider range of contexts than ever before. There is no single charismatic Pied-Piper figure leading a vanguard of younger poets, but distinctive voices are emerging from the pages of literary periodicals and student publications, and appearing in handsome first and subsequent collections. Most of these younger poets are also committed to bringing their work to as wide an audience as possible, and are enthusiastic participators in (and organisers of) Irish-language and dual-language poetry festivals and literary events. There is no dedicated Irish-language poetry publisher, yet all the main publishing houses publish poetry, with Coiscéim being the most frequent outlet for first and new collections, while publishing houses such as Gallery, Dedalus, and Arlen House publish Irish-language poetry in dual-language format.

The geographically dispersed and mobile community of poets represented in this volume have certainly benefitted from the communication advances associated with the digital age, and one development in particular coincided with their recent emergence as published authors. In 2007, Ríona Nic Congáil, a young literary scholar and critic and author of books for children, identified a need for a supportive network for emerging young writers in Irish, and she established Cumann na Scríbhneoirí Óga (the Young Writers' Association), subsequently changing the title to Cumann na Scríbhneoirí Úra (the New Writers' Association). The association was active until 2012, during which period poets Aifric Mac Aodha, Ailbhe Ní Ghearbhuigh, Caitríona Ní Chléirchín, Simon Ó Faoláin, and

Doireann Ní Ghríofa, all loosely affiliated with it, were to publish their first collections. Proinsias Mac a' Bhaird, another affiliate, had already published his first collection, *Idir Beocht agus Beatha*, in 2004. In 2008 the publishing house Cois Life, in response to the Scríbhneoirí Úra initiative, and as part of their policy of promoting new authors, published a selection of prose and poetry *Blaiseadh Pinn: Nuascríbhneoireacht Ghaeilge*, which included poems by Ailbhe Ní Ghearbhuigh, Caitríona Ní Chléirchín, and Simon Ó Faoláin. When Nic Congáil guest-edited two special 'Scríbhneoirí Úra' editions of the monthly magazine *Comhar* (in October 2009 and September 2010), the contributors again included Aifric Mac Aodha, Ailbhe Ní Ghearbhuigh, Caitríona Ní Chléirchín, Simon Ó Faoláin, and Proinsias Mac a' Bhaird (all of whom contributed to both special editions) and Doireann Ní Ghríofa (who contributed to the September 2010 edition).

Though I believe that these poets would have made their mark individually in any case, I think their emergence as a new grouping was given momentum by the Scríbhneoirí Úra initiative, resulting in a clustering of publishing activity in the ten-year period 2008-2018. A listing of the collections of seven of the poets in *Calling Cards* tells its own story: Caitríona Ní Chléirchín, *Crithloinnir* (Coiscéim, 2010), *An Bhrídeach Sí* (Coiscéim, 2014); Ailbhe Ní Ghearbhuigh, *Péacadh* (Coiscéim, 2008), *Tost agus Allagar* (Coiscéim, 2016), and the dual-language *The Coast Road* (The Gallery Press, 2016); Doireann Ní Ghríofa, *Résheoid* (Coiscéim, 2011), *Dúlasair* (Coiscéim, 2012), the English-language *Clasp* (Dedalus Press, 2015), *Oighear* (Coiscéim, 2017), and the dual-language *Lies* (Dedalus Press, 2018); Aifric Mac Aodha, *Gabháil Syrinx* (An Sagart, 2010), and the dual-language *Foreign News* (The Gallery Press, 2017); Proinsias Mac a' Bhaird, *Idir Beocht agus Beatha* (Coiscéim, 2004), *Faigh Greim ar an Ghrian* (Coiscéim, 2010), *Bealach na Mine Buí* (Coiscéim, 2015); Marcus Mac Conghail, *Ceol Baile: Dánta agus Amhráin* (Coiscéim, 2014); Simon Ó Faoláin, *Anam Mhadra* (Coiscéim, 2008), *As Gaineamh* (Coiscéim, 2011), *Fé Sholas Luaineach* (Coiscéim, 2014), and *An Corrmhíol* (Coiscéim, 2018), a translation of *A' Mheanbhchuileag* from the Scots Gaelic of Fearghas MacFhionnlaigh. Each of these poets is richly deserving of inclusion in any anthology of contemporary Irish poetry. They are joined in *Calling Cards* by Caitlín Nic Íomhair, Stiofán Ó hIfearnáin, and Máirtín Coilféir, whose first collections have yet to appear. One could quibble about whether other emerging voices should have been included, and one absence that certainly comes to mind is that of Séamus Barra Ó Súilleabháin, whose *Beatha Dhónaill Dhuibh* (Cló Iar-Chonnacht, 2016) is an impressive first collection from someone who has been making a name for himself on spoken-word poetry circuits.

The task of choosing which poems to include must have been an agonising one for co-editors Peter Fallon and Aifric Mac Aodha (with Peter Fallon alone responsible for choosing excerpts from Mac Aodha's work), but the decision to include four poems by each poet was a judicious one, as it gives readers some sense of the scope and style of each individual contributor. The translations by a dream team of poet-translators make the volume a feast for the dual-language reader, and a truly rewarding linguistic and poetic bridge for those less confident in their Irish-language reading ability.

The collection opens with a selection from the youngest female contributor, Caitlín Nic Íomhair, all finely-wrought dramatisations of emotion and conviction. 'Mol an Óige' (translated by Colette Bryce as 'Praise the Young') is set in the youthful milieu of a university campus, where sexual expectations and insecurities are played out in dramas of display and concealment, anticipation and disillusionment. The speaker is sympathetic and knowing, implicated in the theatrics of the scene, and daring only to address those being observed 'faoi m'anáil' ('under my breath'). Despite this self-avowed muteness, however, the poem ends dramatically and emphatically with a disquieting image of self-immolation:

> is faoi m'anáil steallaim orthu mo ghean
> gan iarraidh is mo chomhairle chríonna –
>
> déanfaidh do ghrá duine eile díot,
> díolaim díomá, dúile, dóchais,
> aonbhualadh buile, aonbhuile buailteach
> aonchuisleach, aonfheolach, agus clástra*fuckin*fóibeach.
>
> and under my breath I pour out to them
> my unwanted affection and past-it advice –
>
> love will distort you into someone else,
> a hive of disappointments, hopes, desire,
> just one beat beating, one struck note,
> one pulse, one flesh, claustrofuckinphobic.

Nic Íomhair's poem 'Daidia' ('Daddy') is a brilliant evocation of the loss of a father and the role of religious faith, or its absence, in dealing with such loss. The poem explores the notion that the ties that bind us to the absent loved one are akin to the experience of belief or disbelief, that in every avowal of absence lies a deeper sense of presence that needs to be processed. This is the only instance in the collection where the English translation falls short, as the English title 'Daddy' doesn't give recognition to the dual meaning of the original 'Daidia' ('Dadeity'). The verbal form 'creidim' (I believe) appears three times in the original Irish, but the question of faith is more muted in the translation where the verb 'believe' is employed only twice. The most significant loss of meaning, however, is in the closing lines where the rich ambiguity of 'an fear seo a chum mé / is a cheap mé / is a chaill mé', where 'an fear seo' can be read as the object or the subject of the verb ('this man I made up / I invented / and I lost', or 'this man who made me / who invented me / and who lost me') is lost in the translation: 'this man who made me, / who dreamt me up / and who lost me'. To be fair, paraphrase would have been necessary to faithfully reproduce the meaning of the original lines, and Colette Bryce is to be congratulated for doing a superb job in translating the substance and tone of the other poems by Nic Íomhair in the collection, while also adhering to the formal line and stanza structure of the poems.

The second female poet to be represented is Caitríona Ní Chléirchín, now recognised as an accomplished poet with an assured lyrical voice. The poem 'Cogarnach', brilliantly translated here by Peter Fallon as 'The Talk of the Town', presents womanhood as tiresome pretence, satisfied neither by attention nor indifference, a looking and a waiting game, where self-scrutiny can result in concealment and self-loathing. This portrait of entrapment is tempered, however, by the opening word 'Uaireanta' ('From time to time') and by the gentle clarity of the ensuing verses. Like other female poets in Irish, Ní Chléirchín often draws on traditional imagery from the Irish poetic and storytelling traditions. Where Nuala Ní Dhomhnaill uses material largely of Munster provenance, and Biddy Jenkinson explores the literary and historical associations of Wicklow landscapes, Mona-ghan-born Ní Chléirchín turns to the traditions of the northern counties. The poem 'Scaradh na gCompánach' (translated by Peter Fallon as 'The Parting of the Ways'), *spoken by Catherine O'Neill (née Magennis), Countess of Tyrone*, fourth wife of Hugh O'Neill, is reminiscent of Jenkinson's dramatic poem 'Gleann Maoiliúra' – from *Dán na hUidhre* (Coiscéim, 1991) – with its evocation of Róis Ní Thuathail, second wife of Fiachaidh Mac Aodha Ó Broin. Ní Chléirchín's poem, part of the 'Imeacht na nIarlaí' sequence of poems in *An Bhrídeach Sí*, refers to Catherine's departure with O'Neill for the continent in 1607, leaving O'Neill's young son Conn behind.

Ailbhe Ní Ghearbhuigh's contributions to the collection include two of her best-known poems to date. 'Emigrante' ('Emigrant') uses the experience of non-English-speaking immigrants in North America to explore the drama of acculturation and the linguistic repression associated with it. Though the shame-inducing language is Spanish (and the context the embarrassment of a young girl when her mother shouts to her in her mother tongue), the universality of the experience is communicated when the young girl's determination to assimilate is expressed at the end of the poem in lines that echo a well-known Irish saying: 'Ní bhrisfidh an dúchas / trína súile go brách', cleverly translated by Paul Muldoon as 'Nothing she carried gene-wise / would ever break through her eyes'.

Muldoon's translation is true to the story-telling rhythm of the original, though for some reason he translated the Spanish words of the mother to English, and standard English at that, thus departing from the original where the implication is that the mother was not a speaker of English. Ní Ghearbhuigh has been well-served by translators – with thirteen altogether involved in the translation work for her dual-language collection *The Coast Road*. Alan Gillis faithfully reproduces the structure and rhyming system of Ní Ghearbhuigh's poem of early-morning love-making 'Grasse Matinée', producing a brilliant rendering of a poem whose soothing effect is based on sound and line repetition (the lines 'Íosfaimid oráistí ar ball' and 'ach níl aon deabhadh', rendered 'Oranges we will soon taste' and 'but there's no need for haste' in Gillis's version, each recurring four times).

Bilingual poet Doireann Ní Ghríofa has been lauded for her ability to expose and explore the strangeness at the heart of the familiar and the domestic. Two of the poems published here, with superb translations by Eiléan Ní Chuilleanáin, address the relationship between life in the womb and the human world outside. Drawing on the mythic image of Deirdre from the Ulster Cycle of tales, 'Céad Siolla Dheirdre' ('Deirdre: Her First Syllable') presents the haunting image of 'an strainséir laistigh' ('the stranger within') asserting her presence and responding, from the womb, to a fearful world of threat and omen. The equivalence achieved in the English version is remarkable, as exemplified in sound and meaning from the closing lines of the first stanza (where Deirdre utters her first syllable) to the last three lines of the poem, where the omen of death ('fiach dubh' / 'raven') is transformed into a powerful life-asserting image:

> Nuair a thuirling fiach dubh ar an leac,
> scaoil mé scréach scáfar asam.
> [...]
> Chnag mise, an strainséir laistigh,
> go fíochmhar,
> cíocrach.

> When a raven landed on the flagstone
> I let a fearful cry.
> [...]
> I was the stranger within, knocking
> fiercely,
> ravenously.

It is tempting to read 'Míreanna Mearaí' ('Jigsaw Puzzle'), with its opening images of the pregnant belly and signs of life before birth, as a companion poem, and the two poems were published alongside each other also in the collection *Dúlasair*. In 'Míreanna Mearaí', however, the strangeness of pregnancy and the sense of communication with the as yet unknown, is presented as prelude to the pleasure of a young mother tenderly making the acquaintance of her 'strainséirín' ('little stranger'). The juxtaposition of these poems bring to mind controversial debates about foetal life, bodily autonomy, and societal attitudes to pregnancy and motherhood. Their success as poems lies in their restraint, as they eschew commentary but leave the reader with an enduring image of the unexpected and the unforeseen.

The fifth woman poet to appear in the collection is co-editor Aifric Mac Aodha. The selected poems are in each case excerpts from poem sequences, an unusual editorial choice in the context of a short selection. The excerpts from the sequence 'Sop Préacháin' (translated as 'A Crow's Wisp' by David Wheatley) are the opening and closing poems in the sequence, which in its entirety includes poetic responses to Paul Muldoon's *Quoof* poems. As stand-alone poems, 'Stuaim' ('Cant') and 'Iarfhocal' ('Afterword') illustrate Mac Aodha's characteristic gnomic intensity, tempered here by an equally characteristic sense of mischieviousness. David Wheatley's clever translation of 'Stuaim' develops the poem's playful depiction of a male-female encounter as a game of symbolic gestures and words:

> Ach anois thar aon am eile,
> níl teacht ná dul ón tosach.
> Ag cóisir daoibh in íoslach tí,
> thug tú úll dó in áit osclóra.
>
> Bíonn dúil agus dúil ann.
> A shonc féin, ba mheidhreach.
> Bíonn diúltú agus diúltú ann –
> *No thanks, I've read the Bible.*
>
> As much as ever now
> there's no getting past how
> she slid with aplomb
> not a corkscrew but an apple into his palm.
>
> There's come-ons and come-ons and then some.
> His comeback was winsome.
> There's no thanks, and no-thanks-but-frisky –
> *If that makes me Adam, then you must be …*

Wheatley's translations are always faithful to the tone and spirit of the original, whether reproducing the matter-of-fact explanation of the derogatory phrase 'sop préacháin' in 'Iarfhocal', or the loneliness of the legendary Conlae as he is carried off in an otherworldly ship in 'Labhraíonn Conlae' ('Conlae Speaks').

The first male poet to appear in this selection is Stiofán Ó hIfearnáin, who is represented by three short dramatic sketches, 'Úlla Searbha', 'Coill Liath', and 'An Mháthair Adhmaid agus a Mac', and by a longer poem, 'Melusine', where the eponymous female spirit, and stories related to her, are seen to preoccupy and disturb the imagination of the poem's speaker. There is an assuredness of style in all these poems, coupled with a sense of the unexpected and macabre that is given emphasis in David Wheatley's translations.

The reader is on more recognisable emotional and geographical territory in the work of Proinsias Mac a' Bhaird. The poems selected here include a loving depiction of the father-son relationship, which plays on the Irish phrase 'Timire Teallaigh', which can refer to fire tongs or, more literally, to someone who tends the hearth. Mac a' Bhaird, the only poet in this collection who was born in a Gaeltacht community, regularly draws on the rural and coastal environment of his native Árainn Mhór off the coast of Donegal. The poems 'Bróga' ('Shoes') and 'Míol Mór Bhreandáin' ('Brendan's Whale') are dramatic reconstructions based respectively on memories of a young man's coffin being brought ashore and of a young boy's fears of drowning. The arts of poetry, husbandry, and distillery are correlated in 'Driogadh' ('Still'), with its images of barley field, scythe and heart-warming 'gloine biotáilte / de dhéanamh na heorna' ('a glass of something/ barley made').

The four poems representing the work of Marcus Mac Conghail display a keen sense of drama, self-effacing humour, and a mastery of visual imagery. The short poems 'Léarscáil' and 'Ráthaíocht' (translated by Medbh McGuckian as 'Guidelines' and 'Lava Lamp') display Mac Conghail's ability to combine images to create startling surreal effects. McGuckian's translations take the originals in new directions, and this is most marked in her translation of the dramatic poem 'An Teiripeoir' ('Visiting the Shrink'), and in the playful intertextuality of 'Silk Kimonos', her rendering of the poem 'Beirt Bhan Óga', which explores male admiration and envy in the face of lesbian love. With its evocation of Yeats's 'In memory of Eva Gore-Booth and Con Markiewicz' ('Two girls in silk kimonos, both / Beautiful, one a gazelle'), 'Silk Kimonos' responds brilliantly to the humour and pathos of the original. The poem and translation are a joy to read alongside each other, as they form a perfect dual-language diptych.

Simon Ó Faoláin is a poet of great range and versatility, combining the scientific mindset of an archaeologist with the concern with meaning of a philosopher. Typical of the tone of his work is the pithy speculation in the short poem 'Ag Cáitheadh', expertly translated by Peter Sirr as 'Winnowing':

Seo linn ag iarraidh
féidearthachtaí éigríochta an tsaoil
a scaradh ó
na cúinsí teoranta
ab áil linn.

Ar an dé deiridh
n'fheadar aoinne againn
cioca é
an cháith nó an gráinne
a scaoileadh le gaoth.

Here we go again,
trying to separate
life's brilliant possibilities
from the cushy numbers
we've settled for.

In the end
none of us will know
whether it was
the wheat or the chaff
that flew off in the wind.

Scientific knowledge and physical sensation are presented as alternative modes of knowing in 'Aimsir' ('The Weather on Mars'), while 'Grá Leithleach' ('Selfish Love') explores human propensity to see in a friend only those traits one wishes to acknowledge.

The last poems in the collection are by Máirtín Coilféir, another welcome addition to the world of Irish-language poetry. The dramatic sequences included here display sharp intelligence and a strong sense of the comic. The speaker submits his actions, his reflexes, and his motives to mirthful self-scrutiny in the poems 'Do Chara Liom', 'Codladh', and 'Goileann Giorria, Gáireann Turtar', rendered to English by Paul Muldoon as 'For a Friend of Mine', 'Sleep', and 'Harried Hare, Tittering Turtle'. In the excerpt from the poem sequence 'Críochfort a Dó' ('Terminal Two'), the individual under scrutiny is a traveller laden with the baggage of self-doubt, who realises that, if she were detained at Customs and Excise, she would have only one option:

'... Cad eile, go deimhin, a dhéanfainn
ach an mianach tá ionam a fhógairt?'

'... how could I hope to evade
declaring the stuff of which I'm truly made?'

This gem of a collection displays some of the stuff of which a younger
generation of Irish-language poets is made. It also demonstrates the art
of poetry translation at its very best. The book is beautifully produced by
The Gallery Press, in partnership with Poetry Ireland/ Éigse Éireann, and
it should be on the shelf of all poetry lovers.

Ailbhe Ní Bhriain
The Muses (I) (2018), Jacquard Tapestry, 200 x 164 cm
Courtesy of the artist and Domobaal Gallery, London

The images in this issue are from the exhibition 'The Parted Veil: Commemoration in Photographic Practices', at The Glucksman, University College Cork, from 12 April 2019 (www.glucksman.org).

Roseanne Lynch
Untitled [Stella 1], (2013)
48.3 x 58.4 cm

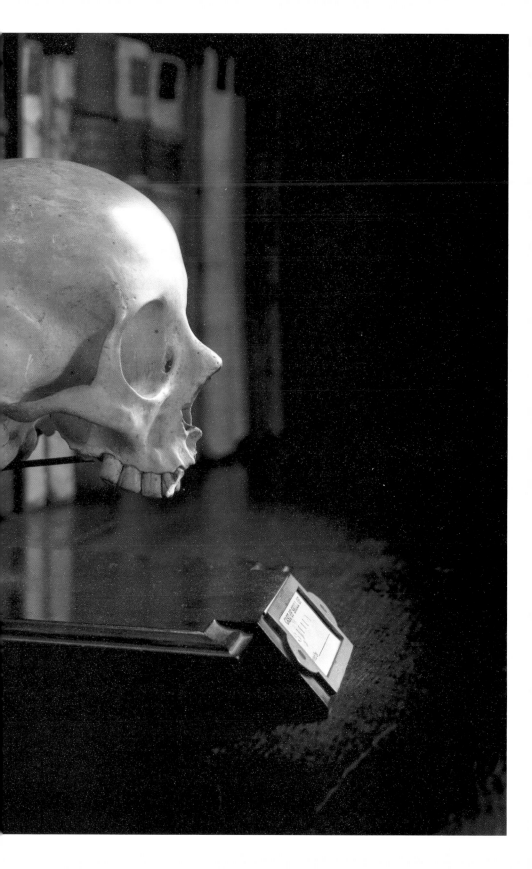

Amelia Stein RHA
Laundry (2018), 57 x 57 cm

John Halpin
Joanna (2018), 119 x 104 cm

David Creedon
Green Kitchen (2006)
50.8 x 76.2 cm

Mhairi Sutherland
Re-imagining Treason (Childers) (2016), 21.5 x 14.5 cm
Courtesy of the artist and the Derek Hill collection

Freddie Trevaskis Hoskin

TO MOST OF YOU

Please
stop
writing
about the suicides.
You are standing in the fields of Flanders
sipping wine in a bullet-proof vest
and your smug survival shines through.
I am sick of your well-loved worldly grief.
I am sick of your manly hands
convinced any words will do.
I am sick of the applause,
the pats on your back,
the badly covered tracks
of your boring quotidian joy.
I am sick.
I am sick, they will say
when it all tumbles down to prose.
And it will,
and they will,
and it will
be
prose,
even though the lines are broken.

FEATURED POET: SEÁN HEWITT

Seán Hewitt was born in 1990. He took his English degree at Cambridge, and went on to finish his Ph.D. at the Institute of Irish Studies, University of Liverpool. He was chosen as one of the Poetry Trust's Aldeburgh Eight in 2015: a selective process that highlights emerging poets. He received the Resurgence Prize in 2017, an eco-poetry award given for his single poem, 'Ilex'. He reviews for *The Irish Times*. And his debut pamphlet, called 'Lantern', is published this year by Offord Road Books.

In a *New Statesman* article on Gerard Manley Hopkins, Seán Hewitt wrote: 'Hopkins is the laureate of "all things counter, original, spare, strange". He is also, to my mind, the most exquisite English poet of the 19th century.' Both admiration and adjectives are interesting. Hopkins is certainly a revelatory poet. He is also capable of wrenching syntax towards a rare lyric honesty, always in the interest of a larger subject.

Which is the strength of Seán Hewitt's three-part poem here, called 'Ghost'. Other poems of his, especially his eco and landscape meditations, such as 'Ilex' and 'Clock' and 'Wild Garlic', have a hint of elegy. The displacement of the speaker makes *place* a poignant destination, at risk of being lost.

'Ghost' is an altogether more unsettling poem. In the mysterious first section, the speaker wakes from a dream and sees a young man outside weeping on the porch 'under a cone / of orange light'. Neither the speaker nor the spoken of is made clear; but both are powerful as mirrors.

In the next section, the experience has triggered memory – his father leaving his house, returning carrying a boy who has slashed his wrists. In the final section, the speaker waits each night for the weeping boy, wondering if he was 'a dream of myself' that yearns to be 'allowed back into the cold room of my life'.

Again, no expansion of plot. In fact, these three sections operate as micro-narratives that gesture towards the powerful question – also asked by Hopkins – of whether the self is an illusion, a projected image coloured by dream and memory, but not graspable and often painfully out of reach. Seán Hewitt asks the question with a deft use of argument, inference, and syntax – powerful tools which bring a complex landscape into focus.

– Eavan Boland

Seán Hewitt

GHOST

i.

Waking, close to morning but still
a shuttered, metal dark in the room:
a sound inside my dream, only a whimper
at first, then becoming human, a howl
raised in the street outside, left unanswered
then raised again. In my boxers, shivering
by the single-paned window, but seeing no-one
among the black shapes of the parked cars
or hedges, I went out half-dressed: shaking hand,
front door unlocked then pushed open,
and by the column of the porch, under a cone
of orange light, a young man slumped,
drunk, sobbing like his whole life
was unfurling outwards into sound.

ii.

And now, I am reminded of one afternoon,
home from school, my father digging out
the root of a conifer in the garden – I saw him
look up, suddenly alert, leave by the back gate
into the alley behind the terraces, and return
panicked with a boy in his arms. I recognised him,
about my age, from school, by his dreadlocks,
his turquoise streak of hair; but now lolling
under his own weight, his wrists draining
over my father's mudded jeans and the patio tiles.
I knew, even then, the rumours about him;
thought as we wrapped and pinned torn sheets
around his opened veins, how we might share,
once the truth was out, a bond, an elective blood.

iii.

Nights later, I only half-slept, expecting
at any moment to hear someone again outside,
as though time might be caught in a loop,
the same boy walking the mapped route
along the dark streets at the same hour
to my door. Again, I unshuttered the window,
stood waiting to see him come, barefoot, maybe,
down the path. Each night, no sign, until I thought,
perhaps, it was only me, or a dream of myself,
asking nightly to be greeted at the threshold,
allowed back into the cold room of my life.
But then, in each of us, a wound must be made
or given – there is always the soul waiting
at the door of the body, asking to be let out.

Heather Richardson

EASTBOURNE

God was found dead at the Winter Garden.
Mortal. Visible. Found by the cleaner
who called the police. Meanwhile the sinners
of Eastbourne stirred from their sleep and arose,
still unaware of their liberation,
except for the chosen few who could tell
by their sense of bereavement, their panic
of knowledge, that today there was no one left
to answer to. They hesitated
at the edge of responsibility,
their definition of the world now ending
not with a full stop but a question mark.

Meanwhile the police had thrown a cordon
around the Winter Garden. Held in God's hand
was the key to a room in a starless
hotel. The Detective Inspector
opened the door and found himself alone
with a sea-view and a single bed.
The only evidence of the divine
was an empty suitcase; no passport,
nothing. The Gideon bible was missing.
The DI walked to the window and saw
the rational grey of the sea. He took
out his pencil and wrote; *The deceased left*
little of value behind, almost as if
he had never existed at all.

Gillian Somerville-Large

A PASSING

The great graveyard in the heart of town
sprouts acres of white stones
marking the losing battle of the departed;

in the chapel devoted to cremation
the walls display more marble
reminders of Protestant worthies;

religion is excluded today;
the choices of the deceased
omit the divine;

after a record of Muddy Waters
we hear grandchildren
read what meant much to him;

from 'The Dead' snow falls
on dark mutinous Shannon waves;
a small boy recites 'Byzantium':

this is no country for old men;
but old we are, and crumbling,
and we will end as cinders
like our friend;

we listen to memorable music,
while the hesitating curtain
drifts over the coffin;

outside dusk gathers slowly
over thousands of graves,
in the distance mountains loom;

are they higher with silver ashes
scattered from Mount Jerome?

John McAuliffe

TEA

Well? I was saying, asking. The laptop like an elbow in front of her,
the phone squirreled into her pocket still peeping out.
The places she is called from might as well be distant
as the town to whose blue mood I return, every year,

with its special combinations of cloud: on the line are delicates
in a yard the rain is on the point of coming for, the river below
rising and no through road. *Back up* ... This picture defaults
to a room which is not all there. Partial, screened, it is hum and glow

and pings. *Tired? Hungry?* Evening's subjunctive moods
colour questions and commands, *either* and *or*
descending from kitchen to sofa and into the old woods
our vanishings are lost on. The bare lawn and sudsy river.

Will we go. Remember parking the car on the pier.
The kettle, the moon. *Come on.* This *will still be here.*

Gerald Dawe

TO STAY FOR EVER: REMEMBERING RICHARD MURPHY

The following is the text of a tribute delivered at Richard Murphy's Memorial Service, Church of Ireland, Clifden, 16 June 2018

I want to start with a longish extract from Richard's prose text 'The Pleasure Garden'. The passage contains so many resonances of his poetry – and his life – that it has always stood out in my mind as an epigraph to his substantial achievement as a poet; one of the finest this country has produced. It is also a perfect example of that 'unvarnished clarity' which Richard co-opted in his poem 'Double Vision', but I'll come back to that in a moment or two. This is the extract, from *Poems 1952–2012*:

> We loved our Pleasure Ground. A great grey limestone wall wreathed in ivy surrounded it on three sides, enclosing us with midges and horse-flies in a seedy paradise of impoverished Anglo-Irish pride. More than a hundred years ago, we heard, there had been a Lovers' Walk behind a yew hedge above a terrace of roses at the top, but all we could find was an endless thicket of briars and snowberries. Below the terrace stood two sentinel cedars of Lebanon, much too tall to climb, planted by the 'General' who had lost his life fighting Napoleon in Spain. Our grand-mother had seen his ghost in uniform standing on the croquet lawn in moonlight. The calls of invisible wood pigeons haunted a copper beech that canopied the lawn.
>
> One day, struggling through hogweed in an orchard just outside the Pleasure Ground, I came across a very old fig tree, and searching under its big green leaves I found a number of small hard unripe figs. After this, the fig tree was mine. I dug, weeded, manured and sowed seeds in the ground beside it, growing Canterbury bells and sweet peas for my mother's vases; carrots, parsnips, onions, lettuce and cress for us to eat. That became part of my 'war effort' against De Valera's neutrality. We ate what grew with no fear of being poisoned.
>
> It was the happiest time of my life.

There's a flow of Irish Gothic here, alongside the self-portrait of the poet as a young boy; the planting and planning and sense of 'doing things', of putting things in order as they should be while shadowed by the grandeur of history and the handed-down versions, the stories of tradition, and the simplest of revelations which pack such a telling punch. 'It was the happi-est time of my life.' Richard's poetry is, in a way, his way of restoring that idyll while knowing full well, such a desire is impossible. His poems are always after the fall.

Let me say that Richard's poetry – its clear, clean lines and 'potent music' (a phrase his pal Philip Larkin used of Yeats); the impeccable diction and story-telling: all these attributes make for a stunning mosaic, almost a ceramic. For these features remind me of those 'two calm urns of white Cycladic clay' which, in his poem 'Niches', 'A woman threw ... lovingly, glazed them in tears / Fired them one sleepless night, and put them here to stay / For ever.' That abiding sense of art being made – 'for ever' – underpins all of Richard's writing. His poems have the anonymity of the folk tradition from which they draw – Irish and English and Greek – and this cool grace is the key to his permanence. Yet Richard's poems imagine things and people and places since his presence in them is implicit and fundamentally unessential. The poem he makes is beyond him and as such will be read as long as poems are read.

Within Richard's poems history lives; the experience of living by and making a life from the sea is made real because artistically present is the reality of that life he treasured – its difficulties and risks but also its folklore and culture. Reading Richard is like reading a classical poet who has pitched up on our westerly shores, and left behind a record of what he saw and did while he lived there. These are poems of equipoise yet there is an undoubted undertow or undercurrent of danger, violence, and conflict which pulses under the poems' glittering surfaces.

> With its loud mouth and sharp tongue the ocean
> Explodes at the quarry-face of the shore
> Without a notion of hearths, lintels and tombstones,
> Gathering more and more power
> To rampage over the island, or disgorge
> Enough raw granite to face a whole new town.
> — 'OMEY ISLAND'

'Explodes', 'rampage', and 'disgorge' sit unsettling as words in the poem as the statues of Easter Island.

There is so much to dwell upon in Richard's poetry – ideas about the 'house' as refuge and shelter, of the exposure of the self in nature, of things made and constructed (from bookcases to houses), of the elusive search for love and affection and how the self of the writer can often feel embattled and craves solitude, the fraught humane and special stories of friends and family life, sometimes jagged, other times hymns of praise, and how the wider frames of history can cast an imposing shadow over everyday life.

Richard's poems – to use the somewhat friendless language of today – negotiate these places and spaces but privilege order and design as an absolute necessity. Think what chaos would mean? His last great book being called *Poems 1952 to 2013* – unimaginable!

When I think of Richard's poems I think of a complete and coherent narrative, shaped and shaped again by his exacting artistic standards. But one that was ever mindful of the vulnerability and tension which hovers at times around the viability of the poet's voice being heard in the present. Richard never lost faith in the necessity of making poems and never compromised on the art required to make poems as fervent and as lucid as the English language he worked within, sometimes with an almost Beckett-like anxiety over each word and its shifting and elusive meanings and tones. Or in, for instance, the monastic-like clarities of the five couplets of his poem 'Vagrant', and its retrieval of just one word in the final line which flips the poem into an unforeseen orbit all of its own, such is the bounty of Richard's sheer delight in language to capture our silences and desires:

> Who is tapping on my study window
> At this late hour tonight
>
> Disturbing the calm yellow pool
> Of light on the unfinished page?
>
> If only it were the fingers
> Of one who will never come home.
>
> Draw back the curtain
> And look your loneliness in the eyes:
>
> Wind is thrashing on the glass
> The scarlet hips of a rose.

Kevin Graham

ELIZABETH BISHOP IN IRELAND

I love the thought of you in early 20th century
Éire, driving around on your own looking
for directions to Gort or Killalea.
You must have been young and quite pretty, gay
in a country that made it illegal to openly love
despite our misty-eyed sentimentality.
Did hugging the coast remind you of growing up
in Nova Scotia? The Irish Sea, St. George's

Channel, the vast Atlantic leading you back
to your beloved New York. How colonies
of birds must have hung beneath your stare,
the choppy blue putting you in mind
of your mother, maybe, her various breakdowns
and subsequent insanity. Poor girl,
with your chronic shyness and fixed self-doubt,
the white sands of Rio and palm trees

of Key West await. So does love, that brightly
coloured bird that flits beneath the breastbone.
But for now there are the Cliffs of Moher
and Giant's Causeway, your giant mind already
heir to a loose control that will win you many
prizes and admirers, although no doubt
you'll always think of yourself as a failed doctor,
painter, architect, composer. Are you driving

to the interior out here, seeking refuge
in the bittersweet north-westerlies? Is this becoming
dream-material? I'm naturally curious.
You cut a gloomy figure standing there
at the edge of existence but I'd say
you were a riot. I love that all of this means less
than nothing to you, that you will always
be at home in another country.

Leeanne Quinn

COASTAL

Tonight the wind in the narrow space
between the buildings mimics the sound
of the sea, creates so exactly the sound

of the sea, it is hard to believe I am anywhere
but coastal. Hard to think of the branches
of these high trees as anything other

than the storm's disarrangement, desperate
to bring the sea inward. If I look out
I might see a city submerged, its monuments

mute in their drowning, its citizens
buoyed beyond care, or thought.
I sleep and dream of human

flotsam, heads bobbing on the surface,
uncharted buoys, marking the perimeter
of a sea where no one wants to venture.

Manuela Moser

TRAINS

Now open the door onto a train carriage in Berlin three years ago
where Annie (my second cousin) is sitting next to David (her husband)
and a couple of friends. The ticket inspector, making his way down the aisle
checking tickets, stops before Annie and David and their two friends

and asks to see their tickets and when Annie hands them over he says
you did not check these tickets at the station, you are meant to check these
at the station. And she replies in German, that she didn't know,
that she's not from here and that she doesn't understand the system

and sorry it won't happen again. But he says you haven't checked
these tickets you will have to get off at the next stop and check them.
She repeats she is sorry, could he let it go just once and she
promises to check them next time, but he shakes his head and repeats

what he has said. When the train stops at the next station he signals
the conductor and waits by the door until Annie and David
and their two friends step down onto the unknown platform and slowly
make their way across the city to the Holocaust museum.

Michael Durack

BIRDHILL STATION

Not Thomas's Adlestrop where no one left and no one came;
nor Larkin's Hull, the three-quarters-empty train gliding
to where sky and Lincolnshire and water meet.
Not the windy, weedy platform of Betjeman's Pershore,
nobody about but a conscript saying goodbye to his love;
nor was it Montague's rain-washed Californian station,
all legendary obstacles ranged beyond it.
Not even Abse's Not Adlestrop, the wrong train,
and a *very* pretty girl leaning out, refusing his gaze.

No, this was Birdhill (Cnocán an Éinfhinn), the right train,
one-quarter full, eight-twenty, no obstacles, wending
from Thornhill to where Pollagh and Eighty-Acres meet.
And students grim as conscripts, heavy bags and hearts,
equations to solve, Wordsworth to learn; downcast eyes deflected
from willows, herbs and grass; the rocking rhythm muffling
all the birds of Lackenavea and Coolnadornory.

Campbell McGrath

AT THE GIANT'S CAUSEWAY

Skeletal heart-ruin, titanic as the vanished elk,
it is, as Dr. Johnson said, worth seeing,
though not worth going to see. Horn-black
mussels bundled at the tide-line, eel grass swaying

destitute above sea slag while cindery choughs
huff and puff like the old steam engine
carrying the landholding farmers to claim
the ancestry of a colonial tongue,

bankrupt since the end of the war and Empire.
Crows and magpies, kittiwakes and gulls,
likeness assures kindred enmity, rival fires
in contested hearths, fallen nests and spent shells.

Blue in the distance the humped soil of Islay,
last Celtic kingdom of Scotland
toward which the rival giant laboured to lay
his honeycombed pavement, island to stony island.

From the cliffs one watches dive-bombing gannets
test the elasticity of that porous bottle-glass,
low hills of Britain to the east,
Inishowen westward, armadas of cumulus

wrecked on the furthest reef-line of eye-sight.
We're in the same boat now, for what that's worth:
the causeway's foundered in Antrim's bight
and giants have passed forever from this earth.

Enda Wyley

WAR, EXTINCTION, AND RAIN

Laurence O'Dwyer, *Tractography* (Templar Poetry, 2018), £10.
Jane Robinson, *Journey to the Sleeping Whale* (Salmon Poetry, 2018), €12.
Nicholas McLachlan, *The Rain Barrel* (Salmon Poetry, 2015), €12.

The air is dank, there is blood on the floor, a head flaps open and a man is held down while his scalp is sewed on. This is the horrifying opening to *Tractography*, a first collection by Laurence O'Dwyer, which offers to the reader, in its initial 'Providencia', a war poem so powerful that once read it is not easily forgotten. The operation is barbaric – 'A bottle of iodine seems to be the only medicine' – and it is difficult to know what century we are in. But then a mobile phone goes off, 'The needle whirls like a starling', as someone, 'Hard to say if he's a doctor', talks into the receiver and we realise that we are in some unspecified modern time, in 'the heart of the Red Zone', where 'Protection takes the form of an incision. / The needle goes back to work again.'

What follows this unforgettable 'Providencia' are poems which O'Dwyer has subtly clustered into sequences inspired by Haiti, Lapland, Chile, Newfoundland, and other places – many of them depicting the horrors of war. In 'Gatereau', we are told 'Compassion is a hindrance here.' The imagery is vivid – 'souls explode like shrapnel', and 'Even the dead are hungry'. O'Dwyer is an engaging narrator, an unflinching witness to war, unsentimental, almost journalistic at times, as evident in a skilled prose poem like 'At the Xaragua', which ends:

> The UN trucks are parked in the dark. The officers from Mali, Belgium, France. They sleep with revolvers on their bedside lockers. The staff sleep outside the walls, in huts on the hill.

Dark though many of the poems in *Tractography* can be, O'Dwyer is astute enough to balance this darkness with a lightness of touch. In the imaginative 'The Monopol Hotel', Hitler and Marlene Dietrich, once residents of this famous Polish establishment, 'are singing alone in separate rooms. / They are crying, but there is a little laughter too.'

If there is some laughter to be had in this striking poem, there is also some joy to be found in 'On Chiloé'. Here, we are treated to a mouth-watering New Year's Eve dinner of 'mussels and fish, white sparkling wine', followed by the roasting of a pig by the sea on New Year's Day: 'we poured vinegar over the meat. Such tenderness and flames.' Joy too is to be found in O'Dwyer's heartfelt appraisal of Art Tatum, one of the great jazz pianists:

It's clear that the amber of a soul is nothing without a fly.
Listen to him play with the smoke in his eye.
The girl in the green dress and the curve of her spine.
Rachmaninov Schmaninov! Let me go blind!

Templar Poetry, founded in 2005, has consistently produced high quality poetry pamphlets and full-length books from new, innovative poets, such as Laurence O'Dwyer. His *Tractography* is an impressive collection from an already accomplished poet whose work challenges and rewards the reader in equal measure.

Journey to the Sleeping Whale, Jane Robinson's debut collection, is at its finest in poems which quietly and effectively proclaim the need for mankind to protect our world and its species. 'Conservation Status, Vulnerable', is short, direct, its message devastating:

Leatherback turtle
sucks down the pale, moon-shaped
plastic bag.

'*Rana temporairia* is Ireland's Only Frog' is inspired by the fact that 42 per cent of the world's 6,000 species are in danger of extinction in our lifetime. This three-part poem succeeds because it rejects rhetoric, gently advising us to 'preserve the species – / thumb-smoothed, rubbed and stroked / to a thin and slippery tissue ghost'. In 'Lament for an Extinct Species', Robinson's anger is palpable. The thylacine, a large marsupial dog, is extinct and Robinson declares: 'I come to this discipline in rage [...] To this / discipline, begging for wisdom to / utter the word *extinction*, I come.'

Throughout *Journey to the Sleeping Whale* there persists a deep yearning for nature to be preserved, coupled with a frustration that this may never happen. 'Sketch Map of a Temporary Wilderness' is set in development land on the Luas Green Line. Robinson depicts a transitory rural idyll. 'To enter you'll pass fifteen bees feeding on ivy flowers.' But the end of this poem creates an ominous scene, predicts the inevitable destruction of this wild site by 'a city planner's projection map'.

There is a wide range to Robinson's subject matter in *Journey to the Sleeping Whale*, and many other poems also caught my attention. 'Baglady' is both playful and witty in its description of what lies or might lie in the bottom of this woman's bag. 'She might collect / doors into demolished houses, / from skips, if they fit in her bag.' Another imaginative poem is 'Radium Mother, 1903', inspired by Marie Curie's cookery book, which is 'so radioactive, they say, / it must be locked in a lead box'.

There is an intriguing dreamlike quality to 'Those who were Seen Dancing':

Come closer now, I'll whisper in your ear

about the day we saw those people dancing
in the street, insanely, to a silent music. Picture
us again, weeping for a beat we couldn't hear.

Oddly, these final lines appear again in a separate poem, 'Picture us again', the last in the book. This is a substantial collection of approximately fifty poems, one that I also felt could have been pared back in parts, with some poems being excluded, in order to allow the finer poems in this collection, of which there are many, to shine. These comments aside, *Journey to the Sleeping Whale* makes for a compelling read, and I can only wish for this first collection what Robinson's book in '*Ex-Libris*' dreams of for itself: 'How I long / for a person to carry me up, open / my body, let sparrow-hawks out.'

The natural world is also dominant in *The Rain Barrel*, a fine and compassionate first collection by Nicholas McLachlan, which uses nature as a means of untangling the complexities of relationships. The opening poem, 'Nature', is set in 'the black ink of winter', where the poet ponders the season but also the sudden transformation of his teenage son into a man. 'How I didn't hear his voice break / I don't know.' The ending of this poem is both poignant and true. 'Much later I realised / his was the voice / of a second man / in a house / where previously / one man lived.'

There is a feeling of a life well lived in *The Rain Barrel*, many of the poems heart-breaking in their exploration of both the happy and fractured states of love. 'In Your Arms' is an honest and tender love poem:

When you hold me, love is nothing else but you and now
and now and you and now and now and now.

Such tenderness is made all the more powerful because of subsequent poems which trace the breakup of a relationship. The title poem, 'The Rain Barrel', subtly makes use of weather to depict the departure of a loved one. 'You left in a downpour. / I watched the rain barrel fill / and overflow.' In 'Merlin', the poet describes collecting his two sons from the school bus, and his own uncertainty as to whether to tell his children the news of their parents' split:

but I couldn't bring myself to disturb the car's
post-school reverie, change the look on your faces
for the sake of a few ill-chosen words,
a story even I didn't know the end of.

McLachlan is a fine love poet and his tributes to family are heartfelt and memorable.

'Jesse', is reminiscent of Sylvia Plath's poem 'Morning Song', for its emotive depiction of parenthood:

> Caught flat-footed as you cannon-shot
> from your mother's womb
> I watched you whizz past my outstretched hands.

McLachlan's other son, Rowan, receives high praise too in a poem with his name as its title, where again we observe a father's tender love for his new-born. 'I lay sleepless in a night swoon / watching your chest rise and fall.' A touching reference is also made in this poem to the late writer and poet, Leland Bardwell, Rowan's grandmother, and to her love of language:

> Look out for the family vernacular on your paternal
> grandmother's side, that lineage of the absurd,
> the surreal and the playful that burns like fire on the tongue.

Other poems in this humane collection excel – poems about McLachlan's own childhood, his troubled relationship with his father, his love of cars, birds, trees, whales and dolphins, travel, and much more. *The Rain Barrel* offers the reader deep-felt poems to return to – poems that are a testament to the varieties of human experience.

Michael McKimm

HOW TO USE THE GARDEN

In memory of Charles McKimm (1848-1907)

For band concerts, military tournaments
firework displays, for Punch and Judy shows,
dog shows, fancy dress parades, for torchlight
processions and funfairs. Use it for performing
Zulus – a rare occasion – for gymnastic
demonstrations, for choral fêtes.
Use it, this August, for a tight-rope stunt
by Mssr Blondin, straight from Niagara,
standing room only. On Easter Monday past
we used it for a Grand Tournament by the 5th Dragoon
Guards, for Lemon Cutting, Cleaving the Turk's Head,
Tilting at the Rings, for a Night Attack
on a Russian Outpost. Use it, if you must,
as the landing site for Captain Whelan's
parachute descent, and for Herr Holtum
the Cannon King, and for a Great Military
Assault at Arms (admittance 1 shilling,
2 for the Grand Stand). Use it for public meetings:
for the Belfast Total Abstinence Society (no refreshments),
the Temperance Association (ditto), the Band of Hope (bring your own).
For students from Queen's to rally around.
Use it for the Great Conservative and Orange Meeting.
Use it for the Ulster Unionist Convention.
Use it for balloon ascents – there's a permanent gasline,
and always a crowd to watch you break records.
And yes, you can use it for walking. You can look
at the plants and imagine America.
You can lie on the grass and decipher the smells.
Use it for moonlighting. Use it to learn about glass
and how we can shape it. Use it to draw.
Use it to dance. Keep it in constant use.

Noel King

PAVEMENT CHALK

When I gave her the packet – excitement,
when she tore it open – squeals,
when the rain cleared – impatience,
when the front path dried – bliss,
when she got on her hands and knees – silence;
like a true grown-up artist,
her blond hair falling onto the concrete.

The loyalist soldier with a great gun
protruding from his fly like a giant penis
was not what I expected my child to draw.

Luckily the rain came back
before her Papist granny came to visit.

Pádraig J Daly

SADHBH AT THE GAELTACHT

She is gone from home,
Leaving her siblings waking to an emptiness.
She is stepping out into herself.

She sleeps on a hard bed
With unfamiliar others sniffling beside her.
She is on a rota for toilet and shower.

She is learning new names for the flowers –
Samhaircíní, nóiníní cladaigh, lusanna an fhalla.
She brings powder of fearbáns home on her shoe.

When class is done,
She chases a sliotar with a stick,
Plays leadóg láimhe;

And, unfearing, in the evening,
In yellow bathing togs,
She takes the wide Atlantic on.

Samhaircíní: Primroses
Nóiníní cladaigh: Sea Pinks
Lusanna an fhalla: Wallflowers
Fearbáns: Buttercups
Leadóg Láimhe: Handball

Sarah O'Neill

WHAT NOW?

Out we came.

Like brand new cars from a garage.

Clean and bright.

Losing half our value at the door.

The ceremony itself was short. We sat in assigned seats in borrowed black veils. Trembling from excitement and nerves, we looked back and waved at family and friends and said silent hellos.

Afterwards, we threw our hats in the air on the cobbles. Full of the feeling one gets when participating in the rituals of any well trodden path – detachment and contrivance.

Crusty students rambled around, hungover and bleary eyed. Like cattle chewing grass outside the slaughterhouse not quite grasping the significance of their vantage point. Careless spectators to their future.

Some wine and photos and then out we drove.

Full of nervous hope.

Aimless expectation.

A nice dinner, a nightclub with no strangers.

A blurry journey home and a sore head.

Is that not enough?

What were you expecting to happen?

Seán Delaney

SONNET TO THE CITY

Hear tumultuous applause over tyre
rubber. Celebrations of natural
zest. Of winged and footed. The fires,
that burn in insignificance will call
the spirit from its tomb. Endless falling
of shoe on path, rubber on tar. Shoving,
honking, racing. Bright bland neon blinding
those who may look up, up along the rooftops
of granite faces, shaved smooth as time will do.
Cherry blossoms marking the first floor, knots
of green with pigeon grey, gone before a bus moves.
Sky and earth framing insignificant chaos.
Moving beyond, into liminality
each soul embraced in violent chatter.

Sighle Meehan

A PROMISE MADE

August and the fading days still hinged
to summer, alfresco living
in the evening I set two places
pour two glasses
fuchsia stems pink and purple
in a sherry schooner
country music, sometimes Strauss
shadows at my table, dance an old-time waltz
sleeves rolled up
daylight goes from the patio
no fuss, a quiet leaving
when the music ends

jasmine air
scent of yesterdays receding
as vespers close to silence,
lilac tames the sun-flamed roses
tucks in their blowsy ripeness
dusk brings peace to colours warring
in the flower beds
darkness watches from beyond the neighbour's wall

I listen to the scurry sounds of nightfall
canticles reaching towards the psalms
of midnight, a prophesy of morning
a promise made before the seas were parted
honey in the crag, oil out of flinty rock

stillness gathers in my arms
sighs a kiss
ruffles the grass, the sleeping daisies
    dandelions grey-blown with waiting.

Philip Coleman

POETRY HAPPENING

Aidan Mathews, *Strictly No Poetry* (The Lilliput Press, 2018), €13.
Mark Ford, *Enter, Fleeing* (Faber and Faber, 2018), £10.99.
Harry Gilonis, *Rough Breathing: Selected Poems* (Carcanet Press, 2018), £16.99.

Aidan Mathews' 'long-anticipated gathering of ... work over the last
twenty years', as the book is described on the front cover's French flap,
begins with a 'Preface' in verse called 'AMDG'. The poem describes
Mathews' development as a writer from primary school to the present:

> Chalk on a classroom slate
> Kick-started the process:
> Capital letters mating
> In a stick insect cursive
> In the shadow of Mother Power

These opening images flag some of the central obsessions of Mathews'
book – writing, sex, religion – and the often overwhelming presence of
figures who (like 'Mother Power') have played a role in the development
of the writer's consciousness, from 'the Holy Ghost chaplain in Butlin's'
('Perpetual Outing') to an 'old German Jesuit / Who survived the atom
bomb in Hiroshima' ('Verges'). Mathew's descriptions of the figure of the
cleric in Irish public life are interesting, but his poems are also pervaded
by what he calls, in the book's title poem, his 'heritage of Hiberno-Latin'.
This is not just a matter of language and subject matter – several poems
in the book make use of Roman Catholic imagery – but it also seems to
inform the poet's view of the world. In an elegy for Dennis O'Driscoll
towards the end of the book, he imagines 'the letters AMDG written
in full DayGlo / At every page turn'. The Jesuit motto (*Ad maiorem Dei
gloriam*) is inscribed in the margins of many of Mathews' poems.

   This might explain why Mathews' poems about sex and intimacy, in
particular, feel awkward, if not troublingly unreconstructed: 'Einstein's
time' is said to have a 'womanly curve' in 'Doing Time', while a 'blonde
schoolgirl picks at [the speaker's] jacket'. However, moments of personal
candour that describe, for example, 'the whiff of my wife beside me in
the bed' ('Eucharist at the Full Moon'), 'the earthen smell of [an infant
daughter's] bum' ('The Berlin Wall'), or 'My father's penis, my daughter's
breasts' ('Menarche'), suggest an interest in the body, and the bodies of
others, that is in constant tension with the figures of 'God the Father or
God the Son' ('Phrases'). When Mathews writes, in the latter poem, of

'the sore ovaries / Of a girl scrubbing floors in Pompeii', or his 'eight-eenth-century heroine / [...] in a tank top / And warm leggings under a mini' ('Sound Effects in a Studio'), it is hard not to imagine him rushing off 'to make the sign of the Cross' afterwards, as he puts it in 'Touch Wood'. As he writes in the book's closing poem ('A Valentine for Ash Wednesday'), whose title summarises the deep conflict between the secu-lar (read 'sexual') and the sacred (read 'clerical') that can be felt through-out Mathews' work: 'My book blackened and went out like a candle / At the thought of the strong scent of their genitals.' There is clearly some 'poetry' in *Strictly No Poetry*, but the flame is faint and perhaps no more, in the end, 'than the day's finessed witch-finding / In those flammable, early-edition tabloids?' ('Strictly No Poetry').

It may be the case that Mathews' work speaks to what Mark Ford calls 'the on- / going crisis in masculinity' in the poem 'Trial and Error', from his latest collection, *Enter, Fleeing*. Both poets are interested in auto-biography and in what happens when one tries to make art of personal experience. However, Ford's poems celebrate process and change in ways that brilliantly capture the sense of 'flight through life' that is described by Walter Benjamin in the quotation from 'One-Way Street' used as the book's epigraph. The book is full of references to writers and artists – in-cluding Karl Marx, Ovid, Tacitus, John Donne, John Keats, Emily Brontë, Thomas Hardy, Jules Laforgue, Allen Ginsberg, Michael Jackson, and Sting – but it wears its learning lightly, as this list itself suggests. While this is a serious book, engaging serious themes, one never feels that Ford takes himself so seriously that he doesn't appreciate the ultimate comedy, if not the futility, of poetry's quest after 'the divine / happiness of conception', as he writes in 'Aloft'.

Enter, Fleeing is a book of recollections and glimpses, and many of them describe moments of palpable pain and loss. Out of these, however, Ford creates a compelling poetic narrative of the self in various states of personal crisis and distress. At the same time, Ford is thoroughly aware of the dangers of succumbing too readily to the illusions of memory, even when it is registered through the medium of the first person. As he puts it in 'Supply and Demand':

> 'Lord O Lord, not
> again,' sighed
> the printer who set
> Henry David
> Thoreau's *Walden*, and kept
> running out
> of the letter
> 'I' ...

The precision of Ford's phrasing here – his meticulous attention to line-length and punctuation – also suggests a certain tentativeness or caution in his approach to things. 'Oh / what a poem – what a poem Thomas Hardy / might have written / about this!', the speaker says in 'A Broken Appointment'. In another, 'Fide et Literis', he ponders 'The cycles / of gibberish swirling / through [his] mind'. Taken together, these poems describe Ford's attempts to navigate the mess of memory, working their way, as the title of 'Fide et Literis' has it, 'by faith and knowledge'. The titles of several of the poems in *Enter, Fleeing* give specific places and dates – 'Nairobi, 1963', 'Lagos, 1967', 'Chicago, 1969', 'New York, 1982', and so on. These serve as a kind of precarious chronological spinal column for a book that is a moving if at times hilarious meditation on the 'erratic, desperate, constrained' experiments of Ford's fractured, fragmented, but wonderfully fluid and life-affirmingly '*fizzing*' poetry.

Harry Gilonis's name might not be as well known as Mark Ford's in the field of popular contemporary poetry, but it should be, to readers on both sides of the Irish Sea, and beyond. For those willing to find poetry in the truly 'little' magazines – in places such as *Oasis, Oar, OBJECT Permanence, Quid*, among many others – Gilonis will already be known as a poet, translator, editor, and critic with over three decades of work to his credit. *Rough Breathing*, a selection of his poems from *Reliefs* (1988) to pieces published online in 2017, contains some of the most original work published in recent years in Ireland or Great Britain. Indeed, Gilonis's first book (*Reliefs*) was published in Ireland by hardPressed Poetry, run by Billy Mills and Catherine Walsh, in 1988, and his work includes some significant poetic interventions in the fields of Irish poetics and poetic history in terms of his engagements with writers ranging from James Joyce ('a song-sing') to Tom Raworth ('Coping Batter'). Gilonis's 'Descant on a Theme by Brian Coffey' brings together a wide range of sources – Virgil, Apollinaire, Pliny the Elder, Gilbert White – to tease out an image that occurs in Coffey's *Advent* (1975). The image describes 'fictive one-winged birds / that fly together as one each lifting other'. Gilonis takes this image and re-works it through a series of delicate syntactic brushstrokes into a text that is both a celebration of the idea of artistic collaboration and an affirmation of this poet's remarkable eye for natural detail:

> each
> by other taught
>
> each
> lifting the other
>
> [...]

at the lake's edge
ringed by winter
all fly together

In this moment Gilonis resurrects the image of the 'ch'ien' bird – having
acknowledged several of its previous poetic incarnations – but his eye is
not focussed solely on 'literary' history. Here, too, Gilonis observes the
natural environment – he is a wonderful observer of seas and seascapes
in poems such as 'walk the line' and 'Reading Hölderlin on Orkney' – but
all the while his work affirms 'the act of poetry, / not the art' as he puts it
in 'Song for Annie'.

For Gilonis, the 'act of poetry' involves conversation but also collaboration – see, for example, 'from far away', his '100-stanza renga' written with Tony Baker – and *Rough Breathing* concludes with a section of
'Acknowledgments & Annotations' that details the many ways in which
his work over the last thirty years has developed and taken shape through
his creative and critical engagements with other writers, artists, musicians,
philosophers, translators, and critics. The book includes a number of
powerful political pieces, including 'foreign policy (a performance text)',
but music is always central here, and there are several acknowledgements
of this throughout, including 'a song-sing', 'Win(s)ter Songs', 'Pibroch',
'for Michael Finnissy', and 'Webern sings The Keel Row for Howard'. In
the end, however, *Rough Breathing* establishes Gilonis's voice itself as one
of the most compelling re-makers of the lyric form in contemporary poetry. As he puts it in 'a breath of air', a text initially created to accompany
the jazz improvisations of British saxophonist Evan Parker:

they were so clear,
those first strophes,
stating
how heart, ears, interchange,
move round:
time's
sequence codifies
all theories,
art
and non-art ...

Ostensibly a celebration of Parker's method, in their form and content
these lines also describe Gilonis's sense of the 'interchange' of 'art' and
'non-art', memory and experience, self and other as they 'move round'
the poet-composer's forming consciousness. *Rough Breathing* is a book
that challenges our sense of what a poem can be and what, ultimately, we
mean when we talk about the art of poetry today. Gilonis's work

unashamedly declares itself as poetry, playfully, often gleefully, recognising both the 'thirst / for the word' ('Win(s)ter Songs') and the importance of being able 'to risk / making / a botch' ('Window, Light Outside'). As it is reflected in 'an egg for E.', here poetry happens:

> closed, perfect, pointless,
> its point must be its
> hatching into the
> potentialities
> of song.

Tim Nolan

In an old room looking South.
I've been here before –

on East 88th Street, on East
9th Street, now on West

Franklin Avenue. I'm much
older now, although if I stop

whatever I am doing, listen
to the traffic, watch the late sunlight

falling on red brick across the street,
I remember completely the close

anxiety of youth, the busyness of my
one mind then. Now I know I'm

of many minds, the least of which
seems to belong only to me.

David Butler

I

Wake to the clang and clamour -
the cowbell and slow glissando
of a tram as its heft glides across
Heuston Bridge, townward.

Wake to the roasting tang –
the old olfactory memory;
the nut waft of bitter hops
over the vats of James's Gate.

Wake to a new day ascending
the granite quays that channel
low spangling sunlight up
the tidal drift of the Liffey.

II

Like something half-hatched
or premature, trailing
the open cocoon along
pavements neon-stained
and uninterested. Like detritus
the street-sweepers haven't lifted.
Like an afterbirth of the city,
stubborn and unruly as graffiti
on its dreams in glass and asphalt.
Like the return of the repressed,
the ghost of the life not lived,
anaemic, persistent as guilt.

III

Return to the cardboard lair,
to its subterranean dank;
to the soiled rough sleeping-
bags packed liminally.

Return to the rumour of wings
under train-rattled vaults;
along the paving, pigeon-spatter
Pollocked autumnally.

Return again to No Man's Land,
to a country of sleeplessness;
return to the greyscale anxieties
that prowl nocturnally.

Cian Murphy

IT'S ...

... the curve of the paved-over quay,
mothers thrust buggy-first in traffic

... *not a bother, would you be well,*
falling from the Farmgate to marinade

... and the Lane as Cobain serenades
a candle-lit crush of jumpers and jeans

... *get stuck in boys, we were haunted,*
at the Park or the Cross or Musgrave

... the Triskel boards when Murphy's
asked: *What's the colour of love...*

It's that.

The penultimate line is dialogue from Enda Walsh's *Disco Pigs*.

Andrea Ward

INNOCENTI
 – for Caro

Today at the shrine of Santissima Annunziata we envied
the candlelit fervour on faces heedless of the sermon echoing
behind them for the feast of the Immaculate Conception.
Outside it was raining again. Sheltered in Brunelleschi's

loggia, we found the window through which hundreds
of thousands of infants were abandoned to the Spedale
degli Innocenti. In the museum we learned her name –
Agata Smeralda, immaculate first, placed on the sill

the fifth day of February 1445, died the following Christmas.
Was it grief that killed so many when their wet nurses began
to wean them? Unclaimed in cabinets, the tokens, fractured
pledges of reclamation, left tucked into swaddling by the stricken:

left with *Maria Caterina*, the top half of a jewelled cross ...
with *Luigi*, twelve desiccated peas on a ragged string ...
with *Attilia*, a blue bead engraved with golden florets ...
Saturnina, half a yellow button stitched to a finger of red cloth.

***

Tonight the umbrellas of revellers below us are spots of colour
moving over wet paving. At our fourth floor window we are
as high over the Piazza as the pigeons huddled floodlit
in niches on the north flank of Brunelleschi's Duomo. And

there she is again, dark-robed, squat under her black umbrella,
trailing a red and yellow shopping bag on wheels, shuffling
past the life-sized crib. By the first pilaster on the north flank
she stops, pulls a package from her bag and opens it to fling

liberalities of seed over the low railing. Pigeons angle down.
Not resting to watch them feast, she labours on to reach
a gothic door whose steps she showers with all she has left
of grain. A deft-winged rabble closes upon her bounty.

She turns away. Hobbling now, pausing for one look
back, she crosses to the footpath under our window
and enters the narrow street where migrant vendors
proffer umbrellas hung like rainbows from their fingers.

Margaret Nohilly

LA SIESTE
 – *for Tom*

I've grown attached to Van Gogh's couple
sleeping in a cornfield, ochre, blue. In them
I recognise our sleeping selves: your
barefoot, flat-backed sprawl, hands lapped
behind your head, hat drawn across your eyes
the way you drop the paper on your face,

cat-napping in the chair at home. And me:
the compliant lie of me, my folded arms
a bolster for your ribs, my elbow snug
in your armpit. Swathed in speedwell blue
to match your shirt, my slumber-leaden thighs
support your loin, made limp as after love.

We're in our early wedded days: for you
enough to have me there – at ease with my
intricate heart. You've planned our rest
in welcome shade; freed the animals to feed;
settled straw to bed us, sickles safely laid:
provident as Boaz to my assenting Ruth.

I'd like Van Gogh to know how well he
captured us: still folded in conflicting modes
not inconsistent with content. I've found myself
in blossom-scattered fields; you lose yourself
in images you hone and share. On levelled ground,
we daily weigh the steady harvest of enduring care.

Seán Hewitt

TUNNELS THROUGH THEIR HEADS

Ciaran Berry, *Liner Notes* (The Gallery Press, 2018), €11.95.
David Wheatley, *The President of Planet Earth* (Carcanet Press, 2017), £12.99.

Both Ciaran Berry's *Liner Notes* and David Wheatley's *The President of Planet Earth* are expansive and varied collections: both difficult to summarise, and both exhibiting a variety of formal preoccupations. In this way, both poets trouble the idea of a 'collection', though Wheatley's experiment is perhaps more deliberate than Berry's.

Berry's *Liner Notes*, his third collection and the follow-up to 2013's *The Dead Zoo*, opens with a meditation on the place of music, memory, and history, the poem's act of 'making a country / so you can walk back into it' replicating the way music resurrects or recreates an atmosphere. The seduction of music is felt throughout this collection (there are poems about *Top of the Pops*, Elvis impersonators, The Rolling Stones, and John Peel), but it is not the poems that deal with music that feel most effective. Rather, some of these poems feel too long, or like exercises rather than poems with an emotional core. They are descriptive, and often clever and punning, but there is an absence of a philosophical or an emotional narrative.

Berry has a talent for revealing a striking concentration of emotion in a single line or image, and it is here that his power as a writer lies. The heart, he tells us, 'is dark and chambered like a gun'. In 'For Shergar', which begins with a scene of horse racing, the speaker goes back into his memory to the day 'my grandfather / / leaves behind the broken stall of his body, / his cancer too a sort of kidnapper'.

The habit of using a similar turn of phrase many times, both in the collection and within individual poems, suggests that a more thorough editorial hand could have tightened them up before publication. For example, the poetic turn of phrase resting on 'all', as in 'It's all guitar shimmer' ('Liner Notes'), crops up repeatedly: 'the band, all Brylcreem quiffs and matching / suits'; 'all flared, florid collar and gap-toothed grin' ('The Hucklebuck'); 'the heart all sediment and sentiment' ('Conventions of the Power Ballad').

The best poem in the collection, 'Shopping in Whole Foods on a Snowy Evening', is a riff on both Allen Ginsberg and Robert Frost, taking in both Ginsberg's 'A Supermarket in California', in which the poet sees Walt Whitman shopping for groceries, and Frost's 'Stopping by Woods on a Snowy Evening'. In this poem, the theme unravels gracefully over a few pages, giving a real lift and depth, moving between the personal and public, the present and the historical, the local and the national, in a style reminiscent of Mark Doty's careful yet expansive work, or Henri Cole's minute unpacking of ideas.

The lengths of Berry's lines here are formidable, but they never feel baggy. It is hard to quote from the poem, because it is all interlinking, and there is no extraneous sentiment, but these lines, which feature the young Robert Frost after the death of his father, give a flavour of the whole:

> ... Later, at *The Evening Post*, the boy will find,
> in his old man's desk drawer, bullets and a bottle of bourbon two thirds consumed.
>
> 'I know San Francisco like my own face,' he'll tell an audience.
> And of his father? 'I trailed him everywhere, in the way a boy does.'
>
> Who's to say, out of such loss, you might not conjure a horse, a man gazing
>
> into the snow, as though it were nakedness, or the broken line down the middle
> of a midnight road?'
>
> – 'SHOPPING IN WHOLE FOODS ON A SNOWY EVENING'

In David Wheatley's *The President of Planet Earth*, there is surely something for every taste, though some readers might be put off by the sheer extent of the book, coming in at just under 170 pages and taking on an eclectic range of forms and approaches. By the end of the collection, it is clear that Wheatley has a formidable talent for speaking in a range of voices and styles. Through translation from French, Irish, Latin, and responses to a range of global writers, Wheatley worries the artificial borders of both language and nation. Adopting satire, lyricism, classical allusion, and writing through sestinas, sonnets, concrete poetry, and a staggering array of forms, this is a multi-vocal and multi-faceted work.

What is exciting and surprising about this collection is the skill with which Wheatley approaches not just a range of subjects and forms, but the way he handles the delivery and holding of emotion and emotional resonance in his work. Sometimes, the poems quip and withhold; however, a page or two later, there will be a searing and sincere piece to overturn the reader's experience. In 'Tunnels through the Head', a sequence of seven sonnets exploring family history, the influence of inheritance, and the natural world, the tonal range and control is astonishing. In the third sonnet, a ruckus breaks out in the house – 'your voice shrapnelling down the phone with / fuck you screams old bollocks face screams I know / your game'. By the seventh poem, the layering of narratives and themes is carried off into an honest and heartrending conclusion:

will it stop here where only the bright stones
and the sea all bare and glitter the sun
on the tunnels through the Head where once but
these days no one but me father coming
and going where only a heron's eye
makes me out and shutting is gone in the
warm close dark is this where you're taking me
far faint last light drowning are we there yet

—'TUNNELS THROUGH THE HEAD'

The ecological sensitivity of these poems, and Wheatley's sharp intelligence, shines through to the last. If there is sometimes an overload, an eccentric and freewheeling humour that undercuts the sincerity of the more personal poems, that is a testament to Wheatley's range. If it gives the overall impression of an uneven volume, that is perhaps due to a demand for collections to be cohesive, both stylistically and thematically, which Wheatley rebels against here. As with Berry's work, a more rigorous editorial hand might have resulted in a smoother collection, but it will be up to readers to decide whether disorientation and eclecticism are positive or negative facets of the reading experience.

Pat Boran

THE OLD YEAR

i.m. Dennis O'Driscoll

The old year has nothing left to lose.
The shelves are cleared, the last of the bread is gone,
and, in the blue-white, ice-cold light, just two
unfortunate school-leavers carry on

in slow motion, setting out in place
tomorrow's miracles – fruit from far-off lands,
vacuum-packed or freeze-dried, seeds and grains
harvested in the great outdoors to stand

like patients in their paper uniforms – and doubt
still nagging us as we go strolling by,
our trolleys like so many gaping mouths
to be refilled. Tonight

your absence is everywhere, in the chill
breath of fridges, in these half-price treats
and Best Before tags. I pause to read
a frozen ready-meal and feel

as faraway as anyone can be
and still be living. And if I push on
with all these luxuries and few necessities,
it is to hear the till's electric song

and picture you, some long-gone Saturday,
the deal done, order once more restored,
your list of items ticked off and filed away,
kids sweeping up, the future at the door.

Vona Groarke

THE WAY MEMORY OPERATES

is the way a man scheduled for hospital at two
at ten plants a rosebush by the wall
and asks not to be photographed
as he tamps the earth with the sole of his boot,
the inconceivable earth.

Small comfort that the rosebush dies,
that instead of roses all summer long
is the absence of roses year on year
shifting a little when the light is cramped
or rain huddles in from the west.

This too is the way I come back
to where I was young and my children were young
to where we planted all those summers
and tamped the months around them, hard

and hard to say where the years have gone
when we lay down, night on night,

when the slipway sings so narrowly
and the wind stoppers up the gap in the wall
and the sky is civil in fits and starts
and the boats play their moorings like spoons.

Tony Curtis

LONGLEY'S WORK

Your books I keep
on the shelf beside my pillow;
slim and strong stalks full
of sap and bearing flowers.

It's right to be reminded:
heed to your place,
heed to your people,
be true to your language.

Yours is not my land, Michael,
or places I have been:
Dooaghtry, Inishturk,
Glen Lough, Carrigskeewaun.

Nor would I recognise
your familiars –
golden plover, greenshank, mallard,
the cloud orchid.

Still, I'll open at a random page
this morning, as I do,
splashing the sleep from my face
with the cold, peaty water of your words.

Bernadette McCarthy

KILMICHAEL CHRISTMAS

Ice dangling from the eaves
of de Valera houses;
winter's comely skirts.

No reindeer or redcoats,
just the pure December glimmer
of low sun, sea of the horizon,

the lost-world glamour
of a monkey puzzle tree
myrrhed in fog

as from house to house I sail.
All is crepuscular edge,
the sharp that makes the sloe

gin sweet, the sorrow
of casement windows
as plans unfold

on kitchen tables, candles
lit to show the way, crackers
burst like mills bombs,

counters wiped down,
shadows soft as a thumb
hunting recipes

off a screen.
I am the stranger here,
the unknown reg

on the high road,
winding out of townlands
in a Michael-Collins route,

marking each way
of these scatterbrack houses
as the Christmas of Kilmichael unfurls.

Julie Morrissy

SQUEEZING THE MUCK

elin o'Hara slavick, *Cameramouth* (SurVision Books, 2018), €6.99.
Noelle Kocot, *Humanity* (SurVision Books, 2018), €6.99.
Anamaría Crowe Serrano, *Crunch* (Turas Press, 2018), €12.
Ross Hattaway, *How To Sleep With Strangers* (Turas Press, 2017), €12.
Liz McSkeane, *So Long, Calypso* (Turas Press, 2017), €12.

SurVision Books is a new poetry venture based in Ireland, with a roster of
award-winning international poets. Both published in 2018, Noelle Kocot's
Humanity and elin o'Hara slavick's *Cameramouth* belong to the SurVision
New Poetics pamphlet series. Kocot is the author of seven poetry
collections, including several with Wave Books in the USA. *Cameramouth*
is o'Hara slavick's first book of poetry, and as such represents a strong
contribution both to surrealist-influenced work, and to more conventional
lyric poetry. o'Hara slavick puts forth a unique poetic voice in this debut
pamphlet, carefully weaving crevices and gaps throughout the work
into which the reader can enter and explore. These gaps also give space
for o'Hara slavick's voice to develop, and for the poems to perhaps give
way to a broader collection. True to SurVision's mandate, *Cameramouth*
features a series of twelve Dada-themed poems, out of the twenty-two
poems in the pamphlet. These 'Dada' poems showcase o'Hara slavick's
inventive and curious trysts with language, evoking fresh images, such as
'the rain of tongue, / the mist of teeth / the moon of voice' in 'A Dada
Love Song', and new aphorisms like 'No one is too young to sound like a
sewer', in 'Dada Digesting'.

I enjoyed the oddness of these poems, which stretched me in a
different way to the lyric poems that comprise the rest of the collection.
At times I wondered, given their experimental inclination, if the Dada
poems would benefit from a more varied form on the page – whether the
use of space might bring forth an even greater sense of experiment. The
remainder of the pamphlet moves between choppy, abstract lyric poems,
such as 'Greek Bus' and 'Red Kitchen', and more narrative and observa-
tional poems like 'Six Gun City', which is amongst the collection's strong-
est. The poem ends with a man driving, 'his gun shifting across maps / in
the glove compartment like an old bone'. Vivid images, such as this one,
bring the pamphlet to life, speak to current issues in US culture, and lin-
ger in the mind. O'Hara slavick has a sharp poetic voice, and a welcome
inclination toward unexpected endings in her poetry. *Cameramouth* is a
promising pamphlet, in which the poet invites the reader to 'squeeze the
muck' with her.

Featuring twenty-nine poems and exploring ideas of community and resistance, Noelle Kocot's pamphlet *Humanity* is substantial in content and range. These poems invoke the complexities of our modern lives, and the difficulties we face in this present moment. Lines from the poem 'Tribute' read:

> Where should I go with my gleaming lipstick,
> A town hushed and no rush of wind. I have
> Gone past indifference into passion with one
>
> Flick of a channel ...

This concern with changing environments, in their various manifestations – ecological, political, and personal – continues throughout the pamphlet. Later, in 'Poem for 48th Year', Kocot observes the 'Live / Sparks that acclimate to this new weather', and an earth dissolving. There are several references in *Humanity* to the seasons, the sun, the moon, water, and weather. Thus, the poems suggest a struggle between the earth and our surroundings, and the impact of human intervention. In 'Tribute', Kocot says: 'It is night now, and the people come in / / From the streets. I stand beholden to the beaches, / Where the authoritarian waves wash out to sea.' Here, the poet alludes to the power of the natural world, its ability to hold us to its movements. *Humanity* is the work of an accomplished poet, and there is a thematic circularity to this pamphlet that allows a sense of urgency to emerge from the poems. The SurVision New Poetics pamphlet series is certainly one to watch in the coming years for original ideas, voices, and approaches to language and to poetry.

Turas Press was founded in Dublin in May 2017, and along with the writers reviewed here, their list includes poets Christine Murray and Jo Burns. In their first year, Turas Press published full-length collections by Hattaway and McSkeane, and followed with three more titles in 2018. Anamaría Crowe Serrano's *Crunch* represents the most formally experimental of the works reviewed here. At a glance, readers will take note of *Crunch*'s various font sizes, graphic representations, concrete influence, and spacing on the page. There is no table of contents – the book begins with epigraphs from Carl Jung and Eamonn Lynskey, followed by a series of untitled poems. There is a break after these poems, denoted by the number 32, and the collection continues from there. I appreciated the non-narrative sensibility in Crowe Serrano's work, and the varied alignment and spacing of the poems serves her experimental spirit. Indeed, the second poem is a concrete representation in the shape of an apple that features run-on lines without spaces in red and green fonts, thus fitting with the collection's biblical themes. The book takes the apple as its main subject, and following the concrete 'apple' poem, the collection begins:

> I was neither Eve
> nor Adam
> in the garden of Eden
> nor the arguments between them
> over who
> and why
>
> I was the apple
> bitten
> tossed aside

As the poems continue, I found myself craving an even more dynamic form, especially toward the end when *Crunch* includes a YouTube link to a two and a half-minute video titled 'The History of the iPhone', presumably in reference to another dominant Apple in today's culture. It appears that Turas Press doesn't currently publish e-books, although an electronic format might enhance works like Crowe Serrano's. I particularly enjoyed the poet's use of forms that require imagination from the reader, such as the poem on page 37 which extends over three columns, encouraging multiple approaches to reading (e.g., across or down the page). Overall, *Crunch* is an innovative collection, which tasks its readers to fully immerse themselves in this exuberant work.

How To Sleep With Strangers is Ross Hattaway's third collection, his first with Turas Press. The title implies a blend of intimacy and distance that is characteristic. Hattaway draws together sometimes disparate influences, including a series of tankas, odes to the Pāua (Māori sea snails), poems about Christian practices, and confessional and lyric poems. Originally from New Zealand and now living in Ireland, perhaps this range of influence follows from Hattaway's own varied experiences. His wry humour comes through in poems such as 'Shopping', which compiles poetic forms and literary references into a routine grocery list:

> Four bags mixed reviews
> Small jar schadenfreude, for competitions
> Value pack clichés
> Family sized underlying theme, for emergencies
> Packet of influences, sliced
> Packet of influences, sliced wholegrain

In other places, the poems edge toward a didactic tone – for example, lines in the short poem 'Nineteen' read: 'Neutral is only a concept / in our reality. / Whether we care or not, / it is hard to stand still.' The collection is mostly comprised of short, snappy poems, with the exception of 'Unravelling the Edges of Speculative Physics', which again shows Hattaway's more playful and humorous side. The title poem of the collection questions our familiar relationships, perhaps probing at the distance that can sometimes lie in the familiar. In this poem Hattaway writes, 'You may have gone to sleep / for years / and woken up / to a new world.' At times, reading this collection was akin to waking up in new surroundings, a slightly disorienting experience, but one with enough intrigue to relish exploring.

Mortality, immortality, and ageing are conjured both in the title and the poems of Liz McSkeane's *So Long, Calypso*. The collection moves between various cities and towns, including Amsterdam, Glasgow, Dublin, Cork, and Kerry, and is punctuated throughout with a handful of poems about a friend named Angela struggling with old age, and a long narrative poem. The form and run-on lines of the long poem, titled 'Visiting Monuments', suits its theme, as the speaker wades methodically through queues, ultimately losing her cherished belongings in the fray of bureaucracy. My favourite poem in the collection is 'Incident on the Prinsengracht', owing to its intricate fabric which brings together evocative images from nature, alongside historical references and contemporary life. McSkeane writes:

> A light lavender breeze rises,
> flutters napkins and newspapers
>
> until, in the middle of it all
> a ragged crane wheels into view,
> drops, lands on the handrail outside
> Anne Frank's attic.

The language in this poem is delicate and moving, and, paired with its strong images, 'Incident on the Prinsengracht' moves outward from the questions it poses, evoking an animated sense of place. The final lines juxtapose modernity and nature ...

> ... as cranes plunge to spear
> the day-old chicks, probably dead
>
> before those gaping beaks got hold of them.

This stark ending shows McSkeane at her best.

So Long, Calypso harbours a lasting charm, and, from the collections reviewed here, it seems that Turas Press too has a bright future in Irish poetry.

Michael Coady

THE BIG RIVER

I don't know what became
of some of the boys
I played with years ago
on the Fair Green

or in the sally islands
skirting the Strand Walk
near Ormond Castle.

Did they go off and join
some foreign war
or were they sent
to Two Mile Bridge
below Clonmel

on account of being poor
and missing school
or being orphaned

or for stealing apples that
we used to call Sheep's Snouts,
from Pearl Beary's orchard
near Dead Man's Boreen
beyond in Cregg?

Or can the shades of some
who are no longer in this world
still play hide and seek
behind the trees
after dark in the Town Park?

or fish the tides
for trout and eels
down where the Lingaun stream
joins the big river?

As for the ones
I still meet now and then
around the town,

or in the pub,
or home for Christmas
or a funeral –

when we cross paths
they tell me I
am looking well,
as though boys

who once played together
are so forever,
even as they bend closer
to catch whatever's said,

like those sidelined old men
you might notice on fine days
leaning on the bridge
and towards each other

when we played hurling
on the Green
and in summer fished and swam
in the big river.

Harry Clifton

ANABASIS

Saint-John Perse, Peking 1917

Forbidden to the city, looking out
Beyond Mongolia, lies the hinterland
Of imagination. Watchtower and redoubt,
The lost Qing dynasties, are grass in the wind.
Gone the binary world of time and place,
The Occident, the Orient, interchangeable –
Pieces in a chess game ... On he plays
With Liang Kichao, with Liu. Already the Stranger

Forms inside him, like a pure idea –
He who writes the book of yellow dust,
Who contemplates the ends of civilisations,
The beginnings ... Of all hours, these the happiest
While the stable-boy from the Legation
Grooms his desert stallion, tamed before the Fall,
And tree frogs, a mosquito off the wall
Perch at his plate, a woman pours green tea

And the epic goes on forming. *Anabase* –
The movement of peoples, after Xenophon,
To and from the ocean ...
                                      Here inland
The north-west wind. She lights the Russian stove
In the winter garden, where a lizard plays
At killing insects, and the War goes on.
Liang Kichao has moved. A counter-move
From Liu Tsiang-tsen. Outside, blown sands

Of plague, oblivion, warlords at the gate.
Tomorrow to set up a quarantine.
Tomorrow Li and his hundred concubines
To be sheltered here, in this state within a state,
The diplomatic zone ... Minutiae,
Duties. Let the real thing grow
Inside, where no man sees it. Lei Hi-Gnai
His chessmates call him. Thunder beneath the Snow.

And some day, come the summer, he will go
Behind the veil of time and history
Where the gods lie around, in smashed theogonies
Of stone, to sleep in the ruins of Tao-Yu
And wake to the human caravan setting out
All over again, forever going west –
The wild geese flying, absence of whereabouts,
Mountain cold, an epic space as vast

As Inner Mongolia, setting itself free.
By the roads of all the earth, the Stranger to his ways ...
The child of an island race, in the Gulf Stream,
Who sees it all already in a dream
(Gone the binary world of time and place).
The horse on the desert route, who scents the sea
And dies inland. The son without a mother
Grown into a man eternally other

Sleeping under the stars, in high Xinchan
Tonight, Beijing in the distance, incoming flights,
Thalassal surge of traffic, avenues of lights ...
Here comes the boy, from the other side of time,
With eggs, a pullet, legends of Verdun,
The boy from the stables, beating a little stone drum
Below by the river, for the ferry across
From Tiananmen Square to Xenophon's wilderness.

Garrett Igoe

WHAT SHALL I SAY ABOUT MY FATHER?

That I never knew him to be wrong
he always had the answer
his military mind
knew the way to go
on those long car journeys west
Kilcock, Enfield, Kinnegad.

That he kicked with his left foot
was bald in his twenties
had brown eyes
freckles on his forearms
one false tooth
and nice hands.

That when we pestered him to tell
naughty things he did as a boy
we never got beyond
his painting a hen green
and hiding behind the blackboard
while his father taught class.

That the journey west was his songline
and when we crossed the Shannon
in Athlone, he loosened up
wound down the window
told us to stick out our tongues
and taste the salt from the Atlantic.

Matthew Brennan

MY FATHER'S COAT

Some days I wear my father's Donegal tweed,
though the silk lining's torn and buttons sport
unravelling threads. He wore it the cold morning
we walked across the quad, surrounded by
the stately limestone halls and Doric columns.

Two backpacked students passed and when one said
hello, my father grinned, flattered they thought
he was the dean, he who had lined our walls
with novels – Faulkner, Maugham, Fitzgerald, Joyce –
the Great Books too, their weight warping the boards,
their substance loosening screws and brackets.

When he was dying, gripped with second thoughts,
he mourned the open doors he never entered.
So when I walk into my morning class
on days I'm clothed in tweed, I'm not alone,
the frayed threads linking me to what the coat's outlived.

Scott McKendry

ALGEBRA OF THE SOUL

Adrian Rice, *The Strange Estate: New and Selected Poems 1986–2017* (Press 53, 2018), $24.95.
Jean Bleakney, *No Remedy* (Templar Poetry, 2017), £12.

Adrian Rice and Jean Bleakney come from a long list of northern poets who emerged in the 1990s and early 2000s but are yet to receive their share of academic attention. Who'd disagree that the quality of a poet's work should be measured in its formal sophistication and capacity for human profundity – what it gets out of us, what we get out of it – rather than on the size of the publishing house through which it's mediated? Unfortunately, obstacles remain between us and an abundance of important poetry: ability, self-promotion, and luck rarely go hand-in-hand, and critics prefer the security of a big press 'canon'.

Fifteen years ago, I chanced upon Rice's first collection, *The Mason's Tongue*, in the much-loved fire-trap that is the Keats & Chapman bookshop in Belfast. As far as I knew then, poems about the urban Protestant working-class (paramilitaries and the annual bonfire) existed only as stethoscopic examinations from without, rather than frank cerebrations from within. Rice observes his native place with candour in poems like 'Sides' where – encountering the graffito 'FUCK THE NEXT POPE' – we contemplate a noxious cynicism, only to be betrayed by our own amusement. And Troubled souvenirs are only one facet of Rice. *The Strange Estate* opens with the elusive *Muck Island* poems from a 1990s collaboration with artist Ross Wilson. Although dispersed throughout *The Mason's Tongue*, I was thrilled to see these in their original order, alongside their Gaelic translations by Brian MacLochlainn and the late Aodán Mac Póilin. The opening poem, 'The Mason's Tongue', fuses surrealism and romanticism with perturbing, delightful results. Here, the disembodied tongue of a loose-lipped freemason gives an account of an esoteric god's indifference. This subject – flopping around 'like an odd curl of meat' – is reminiscent of a Desmond Morris polyp, whilst its refrain channels James Clarence Mangan: '*Go tell all the brethren*', it announces, '*There is no rest where I have gone, / No answer comes from Jah-Bul-On*'. From this 'antique land' to its final poem (a comedy of eejits, where two twentieth-century city-slicking amateurs attempt to rescue a sick pig), *Muck Island* historicises (and mythicises) the drab greys and piercing greens of the Islandmagee peninsula, conjuring a hitherto untapped Co Antrim gothic.

There's an obsession with ascetic innerness across Rice's oeuvre. The SMS lends its form to the lyric in 'Texts' where, in a late-night message to his friend, Alan Mearns, the speaker writes: 'It doesn't matter how vast it is "out there". / We all know the "in here" is vaster.' At its core, *The Strange Estate* showcases a poetic imbued with migration and transcendence. Indeed, the poet himself settled in Hickory, North Carolina over a decade ago, and although his 'American' poems are populated with scrutinised flora and fauna, these are 'background comfort[s]' for a consciousness that's never left the primal scene of 1960s Belfast, where the boy on the scullery floor's amazed to simply *be*. There's a caustic poignancy at the heart of Rice's poetic where it utters the human certainty that 'Everything's a preparation for separation', especially when paired with the caveat, 'life's only ever really good, if it's good for you'. In 'Neighbourhood', Belfast squares up to white-fenced Carolinian avenues. Sipping 'chilled wine' to the 'evening fugue' of 'cicadas', the speaker recalls his childhood, where a neighbour might have asked, '*Who the fuck are you lookin' at?*' Instances such as this embody Seamus Heaney's characterisation of Rice's work: 'I like and admire the way his district and his diction are so artfully tongue-in-cheek and hand-in-glove.' If you didn't buy *The Clock Flower,* you might buy *The Strange Estate* just to read the devastating and witty 'Moongate Sonnets' – a crown *in memoriam* for Rice's dearly departed friend, Billy Montgomery; or indeed, to read the clutch of new poems, which promises even more from a voice which ever aligns itself with the primordial fire '[a]gainst the inevitable dark'.

No Remedy dissects personal and national nostalgias and leaves them on the slab, bleeding. Like Rice, Bleakney's prone to philosophical meditations which rely on the uncanniness of the ordinary. 'Bear in Mind' for instance, entreats readers/listeners to salvage a stray helium balloon from the rain (if the opportunity arises) and let it bob about their living-room in order that they revel in 'second chances' and 'Learn / about physics'. This fourth collection continues Bleakney's lust for classification and taxonomy, which invariably manifests itself in poems about flowers. Lifting down one of her books, I never think I'll enjoy these botanical meanderings – as when I switch over to *Country File* of a Sunday, only to sit transfixed for the duration – but she never disappoints. In 'Forest Flame, Joseph's Coat & The Handkerchief Tree', species are discussed with the gusto of a scandalous Regency drama. We're informed, for instance, that although *Populus candicans* is popularly misidentified as the 'Handkerchief Tree', it's an impostor, a flimflammer – the rightful Handkerchief Tree being *Davidia involucrata*! And *Pieris fortunei* is styled as the

> Survivor of the winter
> that felled the palm trees. The only
> challenges to its worthiness: late frosts
> and snobbery; too loud, too common.

Bleakney's a master of ordering. Following this playful archness comes the easy-going 'Questions in the Plant Area', a poem comprised of ludicrous garden-centre customer queries – 'Have you any "gonnerea"?', 'Where's the herbs?', 'Are any of the men about?' – which are, appropriately, as exhausting to read as they are hilarious.

No Remedy builds towards a crescendo of four poems. The first of these, 'This is Ireland, Sean', is a *tour de force*, recounting the mythology around John Ford's *The Quiet Man* (1952), from its adaptation of Maurice Walsh's short story through its production to its reception – capturing, in verse, history's cultural reproduction of itself. A prose poem, 'This is Ireland, Sean' wears its lyricised research like an oversized ulster but, ever dexterous, Bleakney builds towards its prosaic style with pieces such as *'Empress of Australia'* (an episode from her father's WWII service) and the prose poem 'Observation' so that – like the frog boiled in the fable – when we reach it, forty pages in, we know we're in good hands. The other climactic poems ('The Square, Crossmaglen', 'The Sunday After Bloody Sunday', and 'Explosion') make no apology for being retrospective 'Troubles' poems. Taking us on a journey from an idyllic early '60s South Armagh to the familiar insanities of a province in crisis – 'civility' and 'kindnesses' to bombs and murder – these poems sing to the viscera of one-dimensional narratives proffered by the north's political factions. Untying loose ends and scrambling for meaning, No Remedy reminds us that whilst there's no cure for our mangled souls, in writing we find a palliative.

In this era of lyrical waggishness, where the Yeatsian centre is held with *hilarious* Sellotape, reliance on irony for irony's sake is fast becoming tedious. Recent events have shoved the menace of fruitless language centre-stage. As we begin to comprehend how post-structural digressions from 'old truths' can fortify the worst rather than embolden (as per their design) the convictions of the best, the solemnity of Rice and Bleakney sounds about right.

Linda McKenna

ANCHOR AND ANCHOR

The cloister folds itself in,
a closed accordion of stacked
pleats; sharp pressed edge
to sharp pressed edge.

Tomorrow the day's wings
will gather in battlefield
stumps and mouldy barley,
disobedient daughters, debt.

Now is the time for the soul
facing window, a narrow
point of lamp light where
God swoops and soars.

And behind the door so secret
it can hardly be seen, yawning,
narrow sleeved girls wait,
goffering irons in hand.

Tessa Strickland

LIGHTS OUT

The slip of a boy on the dormitory bed is my brother.
He sits cross-legged, reading in the moonlight.
The aerogram he holds is from our mother.

Hers is a child's hand, each word a cube of sugar,
A crumb of sweetness in the winter night,
Dear to the boy on the narrow bed; dear to my brother.

The monk who chooses night duty is the housemaster.
He stands at prayer, waiting in the moonlight.
He twists his rosary, praising the Holy Mother.

'Who, who?' the owls of Friary Wood call to each other.
There is nowhere to hide in the moonlight.
The master makes his move, swoops on my brother.

Now there's a fight, the mouth of the boy smothered
By the monk's hand, his body a daguerreotype
In the raging dark. Where is the mother?

The body breaks; the soul turns to scrap in the moonlight.
The boy who lies on the infirmary bed is my brother.
He cannot tell what happened to our mother.

ACCORDING TO KAVANAGH

In July 1962, Patrick Kavanagh announced the arrival of a new
magazine in *The Irish Press*. It was to be called *Poetry Ireland*. The
editor would be John Jordan. In his article, Kavanagh dismissed the
notion that 'we Irish are a most poetic people'. He went on: 'In our
own tin-pot way there is a disbelief that poetry has any value.' More
than half a century later, what has changed? How do we value poetry
in Ireland? If there is change, what caused it? Can an Irish poet now
be more confident of a respectful hearing than Kavanagh seemed to
think they could be in 1962?

– Eavan Boland

TARA BERGIN

I'd say many of us would still be wary of claiming that 'we Irish are a
most poetic people', whether we secretly think it or not. I am tempted to
secretly think it because of the way that language is used in Ireland, but
that's my own take on what poetry is all about. Either way, it's difficult
to talk in general terms about the taste of a whole nation. On the other
hand, it's difficult to imagine a poet today saying that Ireland doesn't
value poetry, which it so visibly and generously does. Crucially, there
seems to be a genuine open-mindedness about what Irish poetry sounds
like; a change no doubt due in large part to Kavanagh's own redefinition
of what could be considered 'poetic'. Seamus Heaney, in his wake, raised
the status globally, as have countless other Irish poets who have revolu-
tionised the poetry scene since. Poetry can be difficult, and many people
still don't like it, but if you're going to give a poetry reading as an Irish
poet, I believe you can be completely confident of not just a respectful,
but an enthusiastic and extremely encouraging hearing.

CHRIS MURRAY

Poets are thought to be romantic and impractical people, 'love trips'.
Nothing could be further from the truth, poets are a pragmatic people
and in some cases – as in mine – a questioning people. I am interested
in the infrastructure that supports poetry, and here I am not referring to
the pulley-system of grants, rewards, and poet-visibility that follows the
market-cycle phase of launch publicity. The 'infrastructure' of poetry is
quite simply the very real bolts and nuts that allow the reader to find and
read the poem, and here I agree with Kavanagh, it is absolutely tin-pot.

We need accessible archives and databanks to increase and enhance the searchability of contemporary and historical Irish poetry. We need long-term data and accessibility programmes that ameliorate accessibility for all types of readers, including those with visual impairments.

It is easy to question the value of poetry when it is perceived wrongly, and I use that word 'wrongly' very accurately here. Poetry requires space in which to live and breathe. The poet requires space for experimentation. The first book that a poet publishes is in effect their apprenticeship to poetry, a lifelong obsession. You cannot make a book until you make a book. If then, as a poet, you are thwarted in the making of your book, then the issue becomes problematic: Where are the spaces where you can try out your work and develop what will become your book? Are you a visible poet, can people find your work – how do they do that?

These are the questions I ask myself when I investigate what is out there and how far behind we are in developing accessible systems that allow the reader to explore the wonderful history of Irish poetry. We are failing because we are not using the tools we have to develop spaces for the thriving of poetry. Does the site have accessibility aids like machine-readable data, visual and/or translatory aids? Are we aware that some platforms do not offer these benefits to the visually impaired and that our journals are for the most part, not accessible in braille? Poetry needs to thrive outside of the market and within it. This is our challenge.

MICHAEL LONGLEY

Kavanagh's poverty is heartbreaking. Aosdána would have been a big help to him, but I don't think it would have stopped the great poet moaning for Ireland. Nor do I quite see him as a Professor of Creative Writing. Perhaps Kavanagh didn't realise just how highly regarded he was – his marriage and his death were front page news in *The Irish Times*, as I recall. The poets of my generation revered him. When Derek Mahon, Seamus Heaney, and I drove south for his funeral, we stopped to ask an old farmer the way to Inniskeen. 'Ah, Patrick Kavanagh,' he said, 'a great poet and a great man.' Is he appreciated any more deeply these days? I wonder. Because so many poems get published now, it's becoming more and more difficult to discover the real thing. Is there a danger of even Kavanagh's achievement being stifled? But true poets will continue to buck the trends or operate outside them, and sooner or later they will be recognised by the plain people of Ireland. Do I really want what the editor calls 'a respectful hearing', with its sense of entitlement? The phrase also evokes people being dutifully bored in church rather than excited or unsettled by poetry. Again, are we obliged to listen respectfully to everybody who sets up as a poet? Calling yourself a poet is a bit like calling yourself a saint. Poets have to wait for readers to identify them. My old friend, the late John Hewitt, once said to me: 'If you write poetry it's your own fault.'

VONA GROARKE

I'm not sure it's worth a poet's while worrying about how poetry is valued. Surely it's my job as a poet to write the best poems I can, not to insist on them being valued or receiving a respectful hearing? Isn't that someone else's business, so that I don't end up in a kind of unbearable circularity of tossing the poem from (private) writing hand to (public) reading hand, where it will surely fall between?

Perhaps I misunderstand the question. Perhaps what's implied is the question, 'Does the poem deserving of respect get a respectful hearing?' To which, I'd answer, 'sometimes', which isn't much help to anyone. (Especially when it's also true that pretty bad poems are also sometimes elevated to the position of social utility. We know they are).

Oh dear. It seems I have no pronouncements to offer, thin opinion on the subject of how we value poetry in Ireland. Anything I could say, I would immediately want to contradict. How would we measure a respectful hearing? By book sales, Facebook likes, re-tweets? No, we know better than that: poetry is not a numbers game.

So, I continue to trust that a good poem will attract readers. Some of them will be careful, engaged, attentive readers, while some will be raiders, looking for a smash and grab quote (more than often than not, for reasons of 'relevance').

I'm glad a literary culture exists here, that there are publishers, magazines, literary festivals, bookshops and yes, readers, and that behind so much of it is Poetry Ireland. And I'm glad the Arts Council continues to support this culture in the healthy way it does – it would be discouraging to have to write into nothing. But the dangers of writing into something are just as real. And if that something happens to be a 'respectful hearing', I think I'll pass. It sounds unpromising and, to be honest, a bit dull.

In a final 'smash and grab' of my own, I reach for Yeats:

> Song, let them take it,
> For there's more enterprise
> In walking naked.

TOBY BUCKLEY

Any number of changes have taken place in recent years which can be said to have altered the national attitude toward poetry. Referendums on our own soil and abroad have inspired a greater sense of pride in being Irish, so many of us are primed now to embrace Irish poetry and the many other things that make up Irishness. But the steady march of STEM-love, and an ever-growing obsession with building hotels, are doing all they can to hammer home the idea that there are more important things to be thinking of than cultural growth.

Who gets to read poetry? Who gets to write it? Not everyone can afford to spend much time reading or writing, and it's easy for circumstances like these to make it feel like poetry isn't for you. And if poetry isn't for you, why should you value it?

I feel like it's impossible to say for sure whether poetry is valued here or not. In some areas, poetry will be valued as an art form that's ancient and new and ever-changing. In others, poetry is valued more in the way you value your 13-year-old dog whose company you've enjoyed but whose impending demise you have accepted. Mostly it depends on where you live, who you know, and how good your Leaving Cert English teacher was.

Irish writing and Irish writers make me feel so much national pride. Despite every reason we are given to abandon poetry, we continue to produce a massive amount. People continue to give up their lunch breaks to listen to panel discussions, and to drive across the country to give and listen to poetry readings. Writing and reading are so much a part of our history that they're almost impossible to avoid, and it seems that's the way we like it.

CHIAMAKA ENYI-AMADI

I think the value of poetry in Ireland has changed as the island has transformed into an economic hub, and absorbed all the perks and problems of contemporary life. There is less 'disbelief that poetry has any value' because it has become more apparent that poetry has the potential to relieve people of the disillusionment caused by modern life.

The meaning of the term poet has not changed but the value placed on that term has altered or – worse – been misplaced. The poet is still the person whose task is to hold a mirror up to the soul of human beings, to nature, to society, to the universe, to whatever lies beyond and beneath the porous skin of the earth, and then to distort that view at times, to show what it could or should be, to make it more relatable, more mysterious, more profound, more worthy of attention and comment.

But that job has now been taken on by a different types of creators and commentators, whose interests may not be in drawing attention to things for the sake of love of language or desire for socio-political change, but rather, perhaps, for the sake of drawing attention to the self, to create a fertile ground for economic profit.

'Gaining influence' does not require the inquisitive visionary attitudes of a philosopher or priest or poet or monk to arrive at a line or image that breaks the noisy silence of the internet for a brief second. The concepts of truth, vision, beauty, and absurdity are no longer solely confined to the mental playground of the poet, or artist – those ideas and concepts are now free for all to consider and share ideas on social media platforms. Accessibility is a poet's blessing. The blessing of social media is that despite our exposure to the loud noise of a multitude of opinions and creations, the fickle, the vapid, the absurd, the unrealistically beautiful, the realistically grotesque and cruel, it all rushes down the stream into the shallows. Accessibility creates saturation, but this is not the problem. The problems arise when people still feel empty despite having so much to consume, still feel invisible, not seen and not heard, not represented.

In short, the poet in Ireland today is offered a 'respectful hearing' because the hunger for authenticity of expression and thought is felt more acutely now than ever before.

STEPHEN SEXTON
Looking through the Irish Newspaper archives for the context of Kavanagh's complaint, and finding the intriguingly titled columns, 'Poet says tourists too impatient', and '"The world is ruled by idiots", Says Irish Poet', and 'The Poets Are Beginning To Get Busy', I also came across a September 1968 article titled 'Poets disagree on Merits of Kavanagh', by Des Maguire. He was reporting on the Merriman Summer School in Ennis, during which Thomas Kinsella and Brendan Kennelly reflected on Kavanagh's reputation, with Kinsella suggesting that he 'suffered from the lack of a living tradition' to sustain him. Elsewhere, Kavanagh himself (I learn from a 1962 *Irish Press* article) said: 'Ireland never had a literary tradition'. I mention these articles because I can't think of any time in recent memory when I've read a newspaper headline beginning with the words 'Poet says'. It seems, as an Irish poet, Kavanagh enjoyed a fairly substantial hearing, certainly in the newspapers.

I'm disinclined to compose a sentence that characterises 'we Irish' in any particular way, and calling a person, let alone a country, poetic, has, for me, the air of an insult to it. I've often wondered about the value of poetry, but like anything else, it's unfixed. What's of no value to the professor might mean the world to the teenager who has, for the first time, seen herself reflected in the world. Value tends to be connected to usefulness, and while I tend to think poetry doesn't have a function, I'd never say it doesn't have uses. Moreover, I'd prefer to think in terms of poems as opposed to poetry. One should attempt to write poems, not poetry, I feel.

I can never tell if a general public cares for poems or not, but if anything has changed over the half-century, it might be that idea of a living tradition, or the perception of it. It certainly feels like a livingness of poems is what's happening at the moment, and has been happening for some time. Perhaps that's the difference. Perhaps, after working on their poems, people are – happily – too tired or content to call up the newspaper and say, "Dennis, you'll never believe the tourists I ran into the other day!"

AIFRIC MAC AODHA

Less than a decade after Patrick Kavanagh took his flither, Michael Davitt and his fellow-students founded *Innti*. Famously, this college publication survived, with a gap, for almost thirty years, ceasing only with the death of Davitt himself, or as Alan Titley called him, 'The Pied Piper of Hamelin'. The *Innti* pioneers, the piper himself, Nuala Ní Dhomhnaill, Liam Ó Muirthile, and Gabriel Rosenstock, had precisely what arts' application forms insist on today – 'audience impact' ☑. Separately and together, the four of them made contact far beyond traditional poetry circles.

The current generation of Irish-language poets (the women, in particular) profit from a kind of *Innti*-indebted positive discrimination – almost fifty years on, we can still rely on a respectful audience. I often wonder if we deserve it. When a *banfhile* appears on stage, having thought her 'costume' through (yellow dress?/ white shirt/ red skirt?), it's showtime. Is vanity incompatible with value? I sent a friend those last sentences and he marked a comment in the margins: Who are you taking a swipe at there? Yourself?, he asked. Yes, myself.

Crowd chemistry counts for nothing in the long run ... and posterity will make short work of hair-flickers, shore fishers, and Sunday painters. For the time being at least, many of our older, short-changed post-*Innti* poets will just have to choke their way through this bad bout of *banfhile*-fatigue while cursing the 'fillies' in private for stealing whatever oxygen comes the way of Irish-language writing, in general. In our defence, we know as well as they do, that the real challenge is to follow *Innti*'s piper off-stage and behind the scene(s), to 'get to grips', as Davitt did, with muddled love and grief:

> Níorbh é m'athair níos mó é
> ach ba mise a mhacsan;
> paradacsa fuar a d'fháisceas,
> dealbh i gculaith Dhomhnaigh
> a cuireadh an lá dar gcionn.

> He was no longer my father
> but I was still his son;
> I would get to grips with that cold paradox,
> the remote figure in his Sunday best
> who was buried the next day.

— TRANSLATION BY PAUL MULDOON

Deirdre Hines

MY ESSAY ON WAR FOR MISS. DOHERTY.

War is a noun.
A noun is the name of a person, a place or a thing.
All wars are nouns.
There are as many nouns as there are people.
A war can happen between two places, like for example, between Donegal
    and Mayo
in the All Ireland finals,
or between Germany and the most of the rest of the world
in the Number Two World War.
A war can also happen between two people, like for example, when some
    one calls you a name
and you call them a name back, and one thing leads to another,
and then there's holy war in the yard.
But for the most part it happens when something that someone else owns is
    stolen
by someone else, like for example,
your book, your country, your religion, your language, your stickers or
when something that someone else thinks up is given to someone that they
    don't want
like for historical example,
a six pointed yellow star they have to wear all the time
even if they don't want to, or a wall behind which they have to live all the time,
or a slum, a ghetto, a stereotype or an unfair blame.
An unfair blame is an example of a weapon of war.
An unfair blame is like a sticker that's stuck on your pencil box and won't
    come off.
Spelled backwards war reads raw.
Raw is an adjective. It is not a pretty one. It sounds sore.
The wounds of war are always raw. Like sirloin steak or mince.
Cows are the victims of our hunger for raw. A herd of cows is an example of
    a collective noun.
Some nouns are proper nouns and some are collective nouns.
This means that there are proper wars and collective wars.
An example of a proper war is the War on Waste. An example of a collective
    war is poverty.
You can find any noun in a dictionary, because nouns belong to the grammar
of the language.
Grammar was made up by a very boring teacher in love with the noun of
    himself,

and who also knew that nouns would be used as weapons of distraction
from the songs of the angels
who do not want us to be like the present class of adult when we grow up,
because they want us to live in the lillies of peace
which cost three ninety nine in Lidls supermarkets
and to forget all about nouns.

Deirdre Brennan

THE LAST DANCE

When I heard that death had taken you
I wondered if he had come to call as before
in the guise of that Latin American revolutionary
who whirled you from the hospital bed where you lay
so ill and danced you down his wild corridors
to the pulsating beat of chacarera and rumba.

After all that spinning and you half in love with him,
your head dizzy as a drowning willow in a river's spate,
a spirogyra of stars in a far constellation,
he suddenly jilted you, abandoning you with sangfroid
in a breathless state hitched to tubes and drips
and the doctors who had fought him for your life.

Now decades later hearing that I have lost you forever
I think of you ignoring a line-up of Holbein's skeletal dancers
as you lay claim to the last dance with your Latino revolutionary
who awaits you in olive fatigues, beret and laced up military boots.
Pain slips like a silk shawl from your shoulders and I see
the infinitudes of your being scatter in the insatiate dance.

Dawn Gorman

ST EDMUNDS, LATE AUGUST

All the endings begin here.
The lime releases a detachment of seeds,
a spin of yellow
to highlight the grass
around Henry Hatcher, historian,
1777–1846, and his unnamed wife.

You used to spin coins on the kitchen table
before I knew about metaphor.
When they slowed, they fell horizontal,
rattled like a fanfare. I liked the alternative
to going round and round.
Now, you fall and fall.

I sit on this bench, watch people
come and go, all the past and future
turning in their heads.
I call to someone's lurcher, stroke its ears,
hear the robin's pebble-on-pebble call,
hold up this fragment of sky with one breath.

Adrian Buckner

NOT QUITE FOR US

For five decades they have centimetred,
millimetred toward the middle of one shelf,
each on a numbered page in a single volume:

an accepted poem, an enjoyed poem,
a thoroughly enjoyed poem,
a commended poem, a short-listed poem;

a long-listed poem, a selected poem,
a paid for poem, a paid to be published poem,
a revised and re-submitted poem;

a published overseas poem,
a published with a line drawing poem,
a published under a nom de plume poem;

a poem of vivid early promise,
a poem about that special coastal light.

Notes on Contributors

Tara Bergin's *The Tragic Death of Eleanor Marx* (Carcanet Press) was shortlisted for the Forward Prize and the TS Eliot Prize in 2017.

Pat Boran was born in Portlaoise and has long since lived in Dublin. He has published seven collections of poems, including *Then Again* (2019) and *Waveforms: Bull Island Haiku* (2015), as well as *A Man is Only as Good: A Pocket Selected Poems* (2017). He is a member of Aosdána.

Maureen Boyle's debut poetry collection, *The Work of a Winter*, is published by Arlen House. In 2017 she received the inaugural Ireland Chair of Poetry Travel Award to research 'The Nunwell Letter' – published in this issue of *PIR* – on the Isle of Wight. She lives in Belfast and teaches English in St Dominic's Grammar School.

Ben Bransfield is a Poetry Society Teacher Trailblazer, whose pamphlet-length selection features in *Primers: Volume Two* (Nine Arches Press). Other publications include *Poetry Salzburg Review*, *The North*, *Stand*, *Magma*, *Oxford Poetry*, *The Interpreter's House*, *Acumen*, *Orbis*, *Under the Radar*, and *Barrow Street* (USA). In 2018, Ben undertook a residency at the Tyrone Guthrie Centre, Annaghmakerrig.

Deirdre Brennan was born in Dublin but has lived in Carlow most of her life. She is a bilingual writer of poetry, short stories, translation, and drama. Her most recent collection of poetry, *An Oíche ar Bheophianadh* (Coiscéim, 2019), is her ninth in Irish.

Matthew Brennan has contributed poems and criticism to *Sewanee Review*, *Notre Dame Review*, *Valparaiso Poetry Review*, *The New York Times Book Review*, and *South Carolina Review*. He has published five volumes of poems, most recently *One Life* (Lamar University Literary Press, 2016). He lives in Columbus, Ohio.

Traci Brimhall is the author of three collections of poetry: *Saudade* (Copper Canyon Press, 2017), *Our Lady of the Ruins* (WW Norton & Company, 2012), and *Rookery* (Southern Illinois University Press, 2010). Her poems have appeared in *The New Yorker*, *Poetry*, *Best American Poetry*, and elsewhere. She lives in Manhattan, Kansas.

Toby Buckley is a trans writer from Donegal, currently based in Glasgow, where he runs a small zine called *Bombinate*. A sample of his work is included in the e-book *Hello, I Am Alive: Poetry Ireland Introductions 2018* (Poetry Ireland, 2019).

Adrian Buckner has three collections from Five Leaves, Nottingham: *Contains Mild Peril* (2008), *Bed Time Reading* (2011), and *Downshifting* (2017). He was born in London, studied English at Swansea, and now lives in Derby, where he teaches at the University.

David Butler's second poetry collection, *All the Barbaric Glass,* was published by Doire Press in 2017. A poetry commission titled *Blackrock Sequence*, illustrated by his brother Jim, was winner of the *World Illustration Award*, 2018. His novel *City of Dis* (New Island Books) was short-listed for the Kerry Group Irish Novel of the Year, 2015.

Harry Clifton was Ireland Professor of Poetry from 2010 to 2013. His lectures were published as *Ireland and its Elsewheres* (UCD Press, 2015). His most recent collection of poems is *Portobello Sonnets*, from Wake Forest University Press, and *Herod's Dispensations*, just published by Bloodaxe Books.

Michael Coady was born in Carrick-on-Suir, Co Tipperary, where he still lives. A former teacher, occasional broadcaster, and self-styled 'lapsed trombone player', he was elected to Aosdána in 1998. His most recent book from The Gallery Press is *Given Light*, an orchestration of poems, short prose, and photographs.

Philip Coleman teaches in the School of English, Trinity College Dublin.

Quinlan Corbett's work has appeared in *Palimpsest*, the Yale Graduate Literary and Arts Magazine, as well as in *Quiddity*, *The Human Touch*, and online with *The Grape Collective*. Quinlan has acted in New York City and regionally, and this spring will play Orlando in Seattle Shakespeare Company's production of *As You Like It*.

Brian Cronwall is a retired English faculty member from Kaua'i Community College in Hawai'i. His poems have been published in numerous journals and anthologies in Hawai'i, Guam, the Continental United States, Australia, Japan, France, and the United Kingdom. Recent publications include *Bamboo Ridge, Chiron Review, Hawai'i Pacific Review, Ekphrasis, The Santa Fe Literary Review, Grasslimb, The Carolina Quarterly*, and *The Briar Cliff Review*.

Tony Curtis is Emeritus Professor of Poetry at the University of South Wales. *From the Fortunate Isles: New and Selected Poems* was published by Seren Books in 2016. His selected stories, *Some Kind of Immortality*, was published by Cinnamon Press in 2017.

Pádraig J Daly, from Dungarvan, is an Augustinian priest working in the Dublin Liberties. His most recent book is *God in Winter* (Dedalus Press, 2015). *A Small Psalter* is due later this year, also from Dedalus Press.

Teri Ellen Cross Davis is the author of *Haint* (Gival Press), winner of the 2017 Ohioana Book Award for Poetry. She is a Cave Canem fellow and a member of the Black Ladies Brunch Collective. She lives in Maryland with her husband, poet Hayes Davis, and their two children.

Belfast-born poet **Gerald Dawe** has published over twenty books of poetry and prose since his first collection, *Sheltering Places*, in 1978. He was professor of English and Fellow of Trinity College Dublin, and founder-director of the Trinity Oscar Wilde Centre. He lives in Dún Laoghaire.

Seán Delaney is a writer from Kilkenny. He has previously written plays, short stories, and poetry. His first book of poetry, *Songs for Him*, is currently under consideration from a number of publishers. His work has previously appeared in *The Runt*, *A New Ulster*, *Idler*, and *Headspace*.

Michael Durack lives in Co Tipperary. His work has been widely published and broadcast on local and national radio. His memoir in prose and poems, *Saved to Memory: Lost to View*, was issued in 2016. A poetry collection, *Where It Began*, was published by Revival Press in 2017.

Chiamaka Enyi-Amadi, along with Pat Boran, is co-editing *Writing Home: The 'New Irish' Poets*, for Dedalus Press.

Dawn Gorman devises and runs arts events, including the reading series Words & Ears in Wiltshire. Her pamphlet, *This Meeting of Tracks*, was published, with work from three other poets, in the Pushcart Prize-nominated *Mend & Hone*, and her work has appeared in numerous anthologies, journals, and – as collaborative film poems – at international film festivals.

Anita Gracey, from Belfast, has written poetry for Arlen House, *Poetry NI*, Lagan Navigation Trust, Community Arts Partnership, *The Honest Ulsterman*, and even on someone's tattoo! She was shortlisted for the Over the Edge New Writer of the Year in 2018.

Kevin Graham's poems have most recently appeared in *The North*, *Popshot*, and *Crannóg*. In 2016, Smithereens Press published *Traces*, a chapbook.

Vona Groarke's seventh poetry collection, *Double Negative*, will be published this year by The Gallery Press.

An avid enthusiast of fantasy epics and history, **David Hanly** has written a number of short stories and poems, of which 'Voices' is the first to be published. David, aged thirty, was working on a screenplay when he passed away suddenly in January of this year.

Kerry Hardie's most recent collection of poems is *The Zebra Stood in The Night* (Bloodaxe Books, 2014). She has published six previous collections as well as a *Selected Poems*, and another collection is forthcoming. She has also written a radio play, two novels, and has recently completed a third.

Daniel Hardisty was born in the UK and studied at the University of East Anglia. His poems have been published in the UK, Ireland, and the USA, where he is a dual citizen. He was recently a recipient of the Academy of American Poets Prize at Boston University. His collection *Rose with Harm* will be published in Summer 2020.

Ian Harrow was born in Bamburgh, Northumberland. He has published four collections, the most recent of which, *Words Take Me* (Lapwing Press), appeared in 2013. His pamphlet *Finishing Lines* (Rack Press) was published last year.

Francis Hesketh was born in Belfast and studied at the Seamus Heaney Centre for Poetry. His poems have appeared in *The Tangerine* and *Blackbird*.

Seán Hewitt is a Leverhulme Research Fellow at the School of English, Trinity College Dublin. His debut pamphlet is *Lantern* (Offord Road Books, 2019). He is also a book critic for *The Irish Times*.

Deirdre Hines, an award-winning poet and playwright, has won The Stewart Parker Award for Best New Play and The Listowel Poetry Collection Prize. Poems from this collection appear in her first book of poetry, *The Language of Coats* (New Island Books, 2012). She has also been shortlisted for The Patrick Kavanagh Poetry Award and The Allingham Poetry Competition, and longlisted for The Gregory O'Donoghue Poetry Competition.

Freddie Trevaskis Hoskin is a queer Irish poet from Arklow. They studied English Lit and Philosophy in UCD. They are primarily interested in short form revelatory poetry. Their work has previously appeared in journals such as *Bare Hands*, *FLARE*, *Impossible Archetype*, and *Hidden Channel*.

Garrett Igoe lives in Virginia, Co Cavan. His poetry has been published in *North West Words*, *The Writer*, *Boyne Berries*, *Irish Medical News*, and *The Irish Times*.

Paul Jeffcutt lives in the Brontë country of Co Down. He has won two dozen awards for poetry across England, Ireland, Scotland, and the USA. His debut collection, *Latch*, was published by Lagan Press in 2010. Recently his poems have appeared in *The Honest Ulsterman*, *The Interpreter's House*, *Magma*, *Poetry Ireland Review*, and *Vallum*.

Maria Johnston holds a Ph.D. in English from Trinity College Dublin. She has taught at TCD, Mater Dei Institute (DCU), and Oxford University, and her reviews and essays have appeared in a wide variety of publications, most recently an essay on Medbh McGuckian in *The Cambridge Companion to Irish Poets* (2018).

Alison Jones is a teacher and writer with work published in a variety of outlets, from *Proletarian Poetry* and *The Interpreter's House* to *The Green Parent Magazine* and *The Guardian*. She has a particular interest in the role of nature in literature, and is a champion of contemporary poetry in the secondary school classroom.

Benjamin Keatinge is a Visiting Research Fellow at the School of English, Trinity College Dublin. He has edited *Making Integral: Critical Essays on Richard Murphy*, forthcoming this year from Cork University Press. From 2007 to 2016 he worked as Associate Professor of English at South East European University, Macedonia. Based in Ireland, he divides his time between Dublin and Skopje.

Noel King was born and lives in Tralee, Co Kerry. His poetry collections are published by Salmon Poetry: *Prophesying the Past* (2010), *The Stern Wave* (2013), and *Sons* (2015). As editor of Doghouse Books from 2003 to 2013, he edited more than fifty books by others. A short story collection, *The Key Signature and Other Stories*, was published by Liberties Press in 2017.

Michael Longley's *Angel Hill* is published by Jonathan Cape. He was the Ireland Professor of Poetry from 2007 to 2010, and his many awards include the Whitbread Prize and the TS Eliot Prize.

Aifric Mac Aodha is co-editor of *Calling Cards: Ten Younger Irish Poets*, published by The Gallery Press and Poetry Ireland/Éigse Éireann. Her bilingual collection, *Foreign News*, with translations by David Wheatley, was published by The Gallery Press in 2017.

John McAuliffe's fourth book *The Way In* won the Michael Hartnett Prize, 2016. His versions of Igor Klikovac, *Stockholm Syndrome* (Smith Doorstop), is the PBS Spring Pamphlet Choice, and a pamphlet of new poems is forthcoming with Periplum later this year. He teaches poetry at the University of Manchester, and writes a regular poetry column for *The Irish Times*.

Bernadette McCarthy lives near Macroom in Co Cork. Her chapbook *Bog Arabic* was published by Southword Editions in 2018. Poems have appeared in journals including *Agenda, Crannóg, Poetry International*, and *The Penny Dreadful*, and in the anthology *On the Banks* (Collins Press, 2016).

Campbell McGrath is the author of eleven books of poetry, most recently *Nouns & Verbs: New and Selected Poems* (Ecco Press/HarperCollins, 2019). He teaches at Florida International University, in Miami, where he is the Frost Professor of Creative Writing and a Distinguished University Professor of English.

Scott McKendry is a Ph.D. student at Queen's University, Belfast. His poems have appeared in *Poetry Ireland Review, Magma, The Tangerine, Public Illumination Magazine, The Manchester Review, Cyphers, The North*, and *Virginia Quarterly Review*. He has a pamphlet forthcoming with The Lifeboat Press.

Linda McKenna is from Dublin and lives in Co Down. She won the Seamus Heaney Award for New Writing in March 2018, the Red Line Book Festival award in October 2018, and has had poems published in a number of journals, including *Crannóg, Skylight 47, The Blue Nib, Dodging the Rain*, and *The Bangor Literary Journal*.

Michael McKimm's publications include *Fossil Sunshine* and, as editor, *MAP: Poems After William Smith's Geological Map of 1815* (both Worple Press). An Eric Gregory Award winner, his poems have appeared in anthologies including *The Future Always Makes Me So Thirsty: New Poets from the North of Ireland* (Blackstaff Press, 2016).

Martin Malone lives in north-east Scotland. He has published two poetry collections: *The Waiting Hillside* (Templar Poetry, 2011) and *Cur* (Shoestring Press, 2015). His Great War-related third collection, *The Unreturning*, will be published in early 2020. He is an Associate Teaching Fellow in Creative Writing at Aberdeen University.

Ray Malone is an artist, writer, and translator living and working in Berlin, dedicated – in recent years – to exploring the lyric potential of minimal forms in a series of projects based on various musical and/or literary models. His work has been published in numerous magazines in the USA, the UK, and Ireland.

Sighle Meehan's work has been published in journals and anthologies including *Poetry Ireland Review*, *The Fish Anthology*, *The Stinging Fly*, and *Skylight 47*. She won the iYeats 2018 competition, was a runner-up in the Over The Edge New Writer of the Year and McLellan Poetry Prize (both 2018), and was a finalist in the The Shirley McClure Poetry Prize, also in 2018.

Julie Morrissy is a recipient of the Next Generation Artist Award from the Arts Council. She holds a Ph.D. in Creative Writing (Poetry) from Ulster University, and degrees in Literature, and Law. She is the first Newman Fellow in Creativity at University College Dublin, where she teaches creative writing. Her debut collection *Where, the Mile End* is published by Book*hug (Canada) and tall-lighthouse (UK and Ireland, 2019).

Manuela Moser's poems have appeared in *Copper Nickel*, *The Tangerine*, and *The Future Always Makes Me So Thirsty: New Poets from the North of Ireland*. She runs The Lifeboat, a reading series and poetry press.

Cian Murphy's poetry has been published in *Envoi*, *The Honest Ulsterman*, *Ink, Sweat and Tears*, *Best New British and Irish Poets 2018* (Eyewear Publishing), and *Counterparts* (Stinging Fly Press). Further poems are forthcoming in *The Lonely Crowd*, *Poetry Salzburg Review*, and *The Well Review*.

Chris Murray's *bind* was published earlier this year by Turas Press. She curates Poethead, an online platform for women's poetry.

Emma Must lives in Belfast. Her debut poetry pamphlet, *Notes on the Use of the Austrian Scythe* (2015), won the Templar Portfolio Award. Her poems have featured in a number of recent anthologies. She is the recipient of an ACES award from the Arts Council of Northern Ireland (2018/2019).

Katrina Naomi's most recent collection is *The Way the Crocodile Taught Me* (Seren Books, 2016). She recently received an Authors' Foundation grant for work on her next Seren collection, due in 2020. A Japanese-themed pamphlet, *Typhoon Etiquette*, will be published by Verve Poetry Press in April 2019. Katrina lives in Cornwall.

Máirín Nic Eoin is Emerita Professor of Irish, Dublin City University, and author of many books, chapters, and journal articles on modern and contemporary literature in Irish. She has edited and co-edited critical volumes and literary anthologies, the most recent being the anthology of childhood narratives *Aois na hÓige: Díolaim Próis* (Cló Iar-Chonnacht, 2017), co-edited with Aisling Ní Dhonnchadha.

Bernadette Ní Riada is a native of – and lives in – Co Kerry. Her work features in *A New Ulster* and in the anthology *Still In The Dreaming* (2018). She is also published in magazines such as *Ireland's Eye, Duilleoga,* and *Little Gems*. She is a prize-winner in the Jester of the Kingdom competition (2017) and the Bring Your Limericks To Limerick competition (2017). She was guest poet at the 'On The Nail' literary reading in 2018.

Amy Nocton lives with her family in Storrs, Connecticut. She teaches Spanish at E.O. Smith High School and English composition for non-native speakers at the University of Connecticut. When not working, Amy enjoys reading, cooking, travelling, and visiting with relatives and friends both in the States and abroad.

Margaret Nohilly is a former primary teacher, based in Lanesboro, Co Longford. A collection of her poems, *April Promise,* was published by Lapwing Press in 2009, and her work has featured in *Poetry Ireland Review, The Stony Thursday Book, Crannóg,* and elsewhere. In 2018 she was awarded the inaugural Padraic Colum Poetry Prize.

Tim Nolan is an attorney in private practice in Minneapolis, Minnesota. His poems have appeared in *The Gettysburg Review, The Nation, The New Republic, Ploughshares,* and many other magazines. His three collections – *The Sound of It, And Then,* and *The Field* are all from New Rivers Press.

Jean O'Brien's fifth collection, *Fish on a Bicycle: New and Selected Poems,* was reprinted by Salmon Poetry in October 2018. Her poem 'Merman' won the Arvon International in 2010. In 2017 she was awarded the Patrick and Katherine Kavanagh Fellowship and was recently shortlisted in the Voices of War Competition run by UCD.

Nessa O'Mahony is a Dublin-born poet. She has published four books of poetry – *Bar Talk* (1999), *Trapping a Ghost* (2005), *In Sight of Home* (2009), and *Her Father's Daughter* (Salmon Poetry, 2014). A fifth, *The Hollow Woman and the Island,* will be published by Salmon Poetry in May 2019. She co-edited, with Paul Munden, *Metamorphic: 21st century poets respond to Ovid* (Recent Work Press, 2017).

Sarah O'Neill is a young, Dublin-based poet. This is her first published poem, having only recently found the courage to start submitting work. She is most interested in autobiographical poetry, and writes primarily about her own, often deeply personal experiences.

Christine Paice is an award-winning poet and writer. She has published two poetry collections, *Mad Oaks*, and *Staring at the Aral Sea*; a children's book, *The Great Rock Whale*; and her debut novel, *The Word Ghost* (2014). Her work has been shortlisted, anthologised, and performed on BBC Radio. She lives in Australia, where she is an acclaimed observer of long grass and driveways.

Andrea Potos is the author of eight poetry collections, including most recently *A Stone to Carry Home* (Salmon Poetry), and *Arrows of Light* (Iris Press). Another collection, *Mothershell,* is due out from Kelsay Books in 2019. She received the 2016 William Stafford Prize in Poetry. Her poems can be found widely in print and online. She lives in Madison, Wisconsin.

Leeanne Quinn's debut collection of poetry, *Before You*, was published in 2012 by Dedalus Press. She was the recipient of an Arts Council of Ireland Bursary Award for Literature in 2012 and 2018. Also in 2018, she completed a residency at the Heinrich Böll cottage, Achill. Her second collection is forthcoming with Dedalus Press.

Heather Richardson is a Belfast-based novelist, short story writer, poet, and essayist. Her poems and short stories have appeared in journals and anthologies in Ireland, the UK, and Australia. She has published two novels: *Magdeburg* (Lagan Press, 2010), and *Doubting Thomas* (Vagabond Voices, 2017).

Stephen Sexton's poetry collection, *All the World and Love Were Young,* will be published by Penguin in August.

Róisín Sheehy's debut play, *Snámh na Saoirse*, was awarded a Stewart Parker Trust/BBC Northern Ireland Irish Language Drama Award in 2018. Her poetry and prose have been published in *Poetry Ireland Review, Mórbhileog Chill Chainnigh, An tUltach, Cómhar, Feasta, Southword, Tuairisc,* and broadcast on RTÉ's Sunday Miscellany. Her poem 'Ar Meisce' is shortlisted for Duais de hÍde/ Strokestown Irish Language Poetry Competition 2019. She lives near Ballyscanlan Lake, Waterford.

Penelope Shuttle's twelfth collection of poetry is *Will You Walk A Little Faster?* (Bloodaxe Books, 2017). *LZRD: poems inspired by The Lizard Peninsula* (in collaboration with Alyson Hallett), was published by Indigo Dreams Publications in 2018. She is President of the Falmouth Poetry Group.

Gillian Somerville-Large has had two collections of poems, *Karamania*, and *Ightermurragh in the Rain*, published by Lapwing Publications. In 2013 she won joint first prize in the Boyle Arts Festival poetry competition. She lives in Kilkenny with her husband, the writer Peter Somerville-Large.

Tessa Strickland has been fascinated by the relationship between music and language since childhood. Co-Founder and Editor-in-Chief of Barefoot Books, she retired in 2016 to devote more time to her own writing and to mentoring emerging writers. She divides her time between Somerset and Co Meath.

Iain Twiddy studied literature at university, and lived for several years in northern Japan. His poetry has appeared in *The Stinging Fly*, *The Moth*, *The Poetry Review*, *The London Magazine*, and elsewhere.

Andrea Ward has worked as a secondary teacher in Dublin and in a school for township children in South Africa's Eastern Cape. Her memoir excerpts have been broadcast on RTÉ's *Sunday Miscellany*. Her poetry is published in *Crannóg*, *Skylight 47*, *Hennessy New Irish Writing*, and *The Honest Ulsterman*.

Susan Wicks's most recent collection, *The Months* (Bloodaxe Books, 2016), was a PBS Recommendation. Her Valérie Rouzeau translations (both from Arc Publications) have won the Scott Moncrieff and Oxford-Weidenfeld Translation Prizes.

Janis Woodgate is an emerging writer from Kilkenny. Her poem `Sink´ was published in the Kilkenny Poetry Broadsheet in 2018, and she is currently working on material for a first chapbook.

Enda Wyley is an award-winning poet and children's author. She has published five collections of poetry, most recently *Borrowed Space: New and Selected Poems* (Dedalus Press, 2014). She is a member of Aosdána.